ART
OF
SMALL GAME
HUNTING

STACKPOLE BOOKS

ART
OF
SMALL GAME
HUNTING

FRANCIS E. SELL

ART OF SMALL GAME HUNTING

Copyright © MCMLXXIII by
Francis E. Sell

Published by
STACKPOLE BOOKS
Cameron and Kelker Streets
Harrisburg, Pa. 17105

This is a RUBICON BOOK, 1973
edition, of the hardbound book
published first as **Small Game
Hunting**

Price: $2.95
Printed in the U.S.A.

DEDICATION

To all woods-loafers, hunters and hikers who cannot stay indoors in the autumn.

Contents

PART IV

SMALL GAME HUNTING WITH HANDGUNS

PART V

SHOTGUNS: EQUIPMENT, CARE AND CLEANING

PART VI

THE GAME

Foreword

This book deals with small game hunting, a sport which makes a direct contribution to big game hunting skills. The relationship between big and small game hunting is seldom stressed, and when it is stressed, it is seldom that techniques are examined in detail to show *how* small game hunting improve big game hunting skills. One cannot be a mediocre squirrel hunter, and at the same time a skillful deer hunter. The two techniques go together.

Of course, small game hunting is an end within itself. There is no more satisfying hunting than taking squirrel in the autumn hardwoods, cottontail rabbit when the first frost touches the upland pastures with its magic, ruffed grouse in heavy cover and raccoon along the river bottoms and swamps. Truly, one could spend a lifetime in the small game coverts, finding the game always worthy of the best hunting skills. They are our best teachers of woodcraft, rifle and shotgun field techniques.

Rifles, handguns and shotguns considered in this book are those which I have found well qualified for small game hunting by personal use. I have followed common hunter word usage in calling all auto-loading firearms "automatics."

I am going small game hunting—you come, too!

FRANCIS E. SELL

Riverton, Oregon.

Acknowledgments

I am especially indebted to all those hunters, woodsmen and outdoorsmen who in one way or another, made invaluable contributions by their suggestions as to what a book on small game hunting should contain—Grant Hartwell, Art Richardson, Pete Gould, Elzie Randolph and last, but not least, Ethel, who always managed to turn out a tasty dish, no matter what kind of small game I brought home for her to cook.

The illustrations in this book are from various sources including several from the publisher's files. On the whole, however, they represent a great many made myself, some made available to me by various manufacturers in the past for other of my books and hence useful again, and a few especially supplied for this volume. For the latter I am grateful to Remington Arms Company, Inc., Rolfe C. Spinning, Inc. (for Williams), Browning, Bushnell, Garcia Sporting Arms Corp., Winchester-Western, Ranging, Inc. and Michaels of Oregon.

PART I

Field Shooting and Basic Hunting

CHAPTER 1

Plinking With A Purpose

When Art Richardson dropped us at the starting point of our hunt near Myrtle Creek, Oregon, there were six miles of mountain, meadows, sage brush and forest between us and camp.

Art looked up across the mountains where a ravel of morning mist still toyed with a peak. "You know," he said, "before we hit camp we are going to get mountain goat shooting, some brush shooting like we have on deer each autumn, open mule deer shooting, and some long range elk shooting."

Sounded like a big order that early June morning, especially with big game season so far in the future, and no mountain goat shooting within hundreds of miles of our hunting territory. Our game this day was actually ground squirrel and jackrabbit. But the day's hunting delivered just such shooting, even though the early spring nip to the air still held the ground squirrel close to their burrows, except on the sunny south slopes where the first tender shoots of grass and elk clover pushed up through the lean shale hillsides.

Art Richardson is a gunsmith and an expert hunter. He makes beautiful myrtle-wood rifle stocks. He hunts deer and elk in season. During off-season periods he hunts jackrabbit and ground squirrel. In his personal hunting arms rack there are at least ten super dupers—.257 Roberts, .270 Winchester, .30/06—sleekly stocked with myrtle, beautifully scope-sighted. This morning, however, he pulled a rifle from its scabbard for squirrel hunting which rocked me back on my heels, a .38/40 lever action Winchester.

I uncased a Mossberg .22 with a scope sight. In my hunting jacket, along with a sandwich and binoculars, there were two hunded rounds of ammunition for it. No ultra high velocity rifles here!

But wait a minute! Did you ever come to grips with the problem of trajectory and bullet drop? Try playing with one of those old black powder rifles, or a .22 rimfire. They certainly bring the problem of long range hitting into focus as nothing else will.

Art had this in mind when he selected this beautiful old Winchester lever action for our first small game trip of the season, though I had expected him to show with a .25/20 or a .25/35 when he told me the evening before that he was taking a rifle with plenty of bullet drop. I know I had big game hunting in mind when I selected a Mossberg .22.

Sometime hunters are prone to forget the basic things of hunting. It is good to go afield occasionally with a rifle shooting a bullet with a rainbow curve, just to sharpen hunting and shooting wits against the day when one is abroad with something more powerful, big game the quarry.

We eased along the logging road leading toward the divide, our hunting jackets zipped up against the early morning chill. Momentarily, as I looked up those long slopes and rock escarpments, I confess I thought longingly of my .222 Sako which would reach out and nip a ground squirrel at two hundred yards, for these squirrels are a first cousin to woodchuck in habit, with the added virture of seeming more canny and shy. They require a degree of stalking skill equal to that of still hunting deer on the autumn hardwood ridges.

My first opportunity for shooting came, not at a ground squirrel, however, but at an early morning jackrabbit sitting on a granite boulder a hundred fifty yards up-slope.

"Purely a mountain goat shot," said Art.

"Purely a fine chance for a miss with a .22," I said, somewhat dubious of the possibilities.

"Let's," as the politicians say, "take a look at the record." My .22 Mossberg rifle was sighted in for 75 yards. Bullet flight over 150 yards is as follows, using scope sights: 25 yards, about one half inch above line of sights; 50 yards, one inch above; 75 yards, on point of aim; 100 yards, about three inches below point of aim; 125 yards, eight inches below point of aim, and 150 yards, fifteen inches below.

A jack sitting upright, as this one was, is at least sixteen inches tall. I looked him over in the scope, eased my aim up about a half rabbit length above him, and touched off the shot. My position was a sitting one, with my forearm resting over a broken piece of granite—rock steady for the shot. Not a breath of air stirred, save the usual thermal drift downslope which occurs at this time.

My .22 snicked spitefully, touching off the echoes among the mist shrouded peaks. The jack gave a limber legged jump and went end over end into a bitterbrush.

Mountain goat shot?

What ranges would duplicate the bullet drop of my .22 rimfire, assuming you were big game hunting in open territory? Art has a model 70 .270 Winchester which he uses on elk quite often when the ranges are apt to be long, across the wide canyons of those Pacific Coast logging burns. Using a 150 grain bullet, the path of this lethal slug above and below point of aim is as follows, to duplicate that .22 high speed long rifle, give or take a few inches. The .270 sighted in to hit point of aim at 200 yards, the bullet would be: at 50 yards, 0.7 inches above point of aim; 100 yards, 3.0 inches above; 200 yards, on point of aim; 300 yards, 10.5 inches below and 325 yards, 15 inches below point of aim.

Let's see how that shot would stack up against the open western shooting sometimes obtained with a .30/06, using 150 grain loading. Sighted to hit point of aim at 200 yards, the path of the bullet is as follows: 50 yards, 0.6 inches above point of aim; 100 yards, 2.5 inches above; 200 yards, on point of aim; 300 yards, 9.1 inches below, and 335, 15 inches below point of aim. Mule deer, elk, mountain goat—the spiteful crack of my .22 rimfire *did* have many of the elements of long range game shooting, elements which are best ironed out before the opening of the autumn big game season when one is called upon to make a careful precision shot across a sage brush canyon, or, when the game is elk, across those long Alpine meadows which those huge deer love.

Of course, in big game shooting there are other factors beside long range precision shooting. While my shot had all the elements of long range big game shooting, it only represented a very small percentage of actual field shots autumn cover presents to a hunter. For that matter, it only represents a small percent of off-season pest shooting. There are other shots equally important, and requiring just as high a degree of shooting skill.

We eased around the bare face of a granite escarpment, then down through a draw where the foxtail grass was a green tracery against the scattering of bronze shale and rock.

Two jackrabbits flushed from a clump of sweetbriar, taking off with those long easy, loping strides which cover ground so fast, but which seem so slow and awkward. Art snapped his old .38/40 lever action to his shoulder, and as the butt touched, the satisfying roar of his old obsolete coal burner set the echoes to bouncing back and forth among the buttes.

Those jacks were running along a game trail through the bitterbrush, angling sharply away from us when Art fired. The rear one went end over end as the other disappeared in the small growing stuff without affording either of us another shot. Examination showed that Art's bullet had taken his jack well back toward the flank, emerging through the chest area, a very deadly shot, and properly placed to have made a kill on a deer quartering away from a hunter.

Two shots: one of a type used when big game hunters reach way out there to make a kill, the other very typical of about ninety-five percent of all deer and elk shooting. Of the two, Art's snapshot at the running jackrabbit was the more difficult, and required much more field shooting skill than my shot taken from a sitting position at a hundred fifty yards.

If small game hunting, aside from being a wonderful sport in itself, is to pay off later in big game hunting, there must be a shaping up of the shooting to that end. That is the primary consideration. A secondary consideration is the shaping up of equipment to conform to big woods standards when you take to the autumn deer trails.

With the first soft warmth of the early June morning sun, ground squirrels begin a cautious emergence from their burrows.

Here we found a caution comparable to that of a wise old whitetail buck snoozing away an autumn hunting season in the laurel thickets. Here is a canniness associated with a big bull elk hazing his harem down from the summer ranges when the first snows of the winter are falling, and storm winds are growling across the mountains. These ground squirrels operate on the theory that out of sight is out of mind. The least movement will pop them into their holes with warning cries which will touch off the alarm system of an entire colony scattered over twenty acres of hillside.

They have a characteristic, however, which gives a rifleman beautiful off-hand practice for big game shooting. Foraging well away from their burrows early in the morning, they stand up on their hind legs occasionally and take a long careful look. When alarmed they take off like a streak for the security of their burrows. But before diving below they pause and sit upright to scan their backtrail. If you are to get a shot while they hold this pose, there must be a precise mounting of your rifle, a quick centering of the crosshairs, and the shot squeezed off at once. From start to finish, there is every element of a big game shot, with the target poised for instant flight, and a premium placed on a quick accurate let-off.

Want to iron out your running shooting on deer? Take those ground squirrels between pauses as they scurry for the security of their burrows. Have something in mind about a better synchronization of sighting and trigger squeeze? Want to take the time lag out of your big game snapshooting? Con-

Closeup of a West Coast ground squirrel, nee Douglas ground squirrel, California ground squirrel, Gray Digger.

centrate on that pause when they stand up to look over their back-trail with that "What in heck scared me?" expression on their faces. If it is long range mountain shooting you have in mind, there are always sections where you can get that type shooting by catching them sunning on rock outcroppings, and piles of dirt in front of their dens—nice two and three hundred yard targets for a .243 Winchester, a .22/250, .222 Remington, .224 Weatherby or some of the hot wildcat calibers. Best though, is taking them field run, with modified deer equipment from sights to rifle action. In this manner you integrate your small and big game hunting.

Riflemen are prone to departmentalize their sport. They separate their stalking ability from their shooting, when actually their shot is on the make from the time they start to hunt until the quarry is sighted. They separate their small game rifle from large, and their sighting equipment, when in reality there should be a striving for a closer relationship.

We eased over a slight rise where a clump of scrub oak and bitterbrush gave us a screening from which to con a small basin below. At first glance it appeared barren of squirrel. Nothing moved in the grass. We waited, our Bushnell binoculars with their extremely wide fields of view, giving us a clear field of the greening flat. Suddenly a brownish head popped up. Then another and another, until I counted an even dozen. The closest was about seventy-five yards, the longest range about a hundred twenty-five. I took an off-hand shot from the sheltering thicket at this one, holding the crosshairs level with the top of his head. At the viscious snap of my highspeed hollow point bullet, there was a terrific thrashing around, and a fluffy gray tail waved above the grass momentarily as I got a clean kill.

At the sound of the shot the place literally erupted ground squirrels. I snapped a shot at a running target at about ninety yards, kicking dust up directly behind a squirrel of aldermanic proportions, then corrected my lead. Next shot turned him around, and a third rolled him for keeps.

Art's .38/40 roared, and I saw a ground squirrel at least a foot off the ground. Then he started working on one trying for a cairn of granite boulders a hundred yards from our hide-out. Third shot he neatly beheaded his target at about seventy-five yards range. Then he got another which had paused at one hundred yards to see what all the shooting was about.

Stack those shot up against the average big game shooting and you find little difference, though the targets are a trifle smaller than the vital area on deer or elk. A ground squirrel is some ten or twelve inches long, rather heftily built, affording a target about four by ten inches when he sits up to take observations—less when he is on the move.

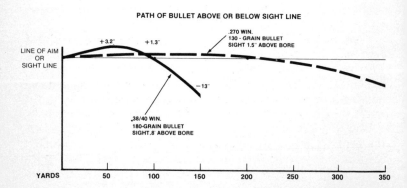

I was beginning to see the point of Art bringing his old black powder, .38/40 Winchester. It had a trajectory curve over a hundred twenty-five yards which very closely duplicated his .270 at the longer mule deer range. His .38/40 was sighted in for one hundred yards. This placed his 180 grain bullet 3.2 inches above line of sights at 50 yards, on at 100 yards, and at least 13 inches low at 150 yards. No room for sloppy yardage estimating here—not if you wanted to connect much beyond fifty yards.

We moved along the edge of the hill, nipping around by easy stages, picking up two or three short range shots. Then we came to a draw cutting into the bare granite ribs of a higher ridge. Here I got two close misses on running squirrels flushed from a clump of scrub oak. Then on a third try at fifty yards I made a clean kill on one going directly away from me.

We could hear the characteristic warning call of ground squirrels all along the broken granite ridge, a call which is very distinct but hard to reduce to paper—"Ech—hit! Ech—Hit!" usually repeated two or three times. It very handily pin-points the game, and also serves the useful purpose of warning us to take it easy because the entire colony was altered.

A squirrel stood as stiffly erect as a Coldstream Guard, about forty yards away. I snapped a shot at him, knowing I had only a split second in which to get it off before he dived for the security of his burrow. Art blasted one off a rock ledge at about the same range an instant later.

We crossed through a dense fir woods without seeing any game save two or three fawns which flushed on the sunny south slope of a heavily brushed hill. These deer went trotting around a hillside for about seventy yards, then paused to look back at us before disappearing in the scrub oak—a beautiful sight, and one reminding up of the purpose behind our small game shooting during the closed big game season.

By the time we arrived across the mountains at our pickup point, we had a sample of every type of big game shooting which might be encountered on the North American continent. We had used the sitting position time after time. We had plenty of snapshooting, off-hand tries. Several times we had an opportunity to rest a forearm against a steadying oak to make a careful shot when nothing more than one eye and a part of a squirrel's head was visible on a rock ledge.

Small game and pest shooting is an end within itself. But it always takes on added rifleman's virtues when it is shaped toward big game hunting. Main thing is not to over-specialize. Sometimes it is good practice to go afield with very basic rifle equipment in order to emphasize the problems of big game shooting. Then, when autumn rolls around, and you are prowling the hardwood ridges with deer on your mind, those off-season shooting forays will pay off with enviable regularity.

CHAPTER 2

Basic Hunting

When Art Richardson rolled that jackrabbit with a running shot at seventy-five yards, it wasn't just happenstance that he and I were easing around that small basin where the first spring warmth had touched off the grass and clover, the tender bitterbrush sprouts. It was sign reading—relating expected game to available forage.

All types of hunting have many things in common, other than actual shooting.

Game from squirrel to elk have identical primary concerns —*warmth, food, shelter and security.* They go about getting these essentials in an almost endless number of ways. But basically they have so many things in common you cannot know successful small game requirements without increasing your big game hunting skills.

Maybe your woodchuck territory will not produce any whitetail deer, due to the lack of suitable cover. But you may be sure that if woodchuck find it attractive, the only reason there are not big game there is the lack of one of the other essentials, shelter or security. Know something of woodchuck hunting from the standpoint of suitable habitat and it is only a short step to knowing intimately the requirements of whitetail deer or elk. Know cottontail rabbit preference in regard to suitable foraging, and you will not be far off in food preference for any browsing big game animal. The tangle of rich food in overgrown, abandoned farm fields and fence rows, coming lush to briars, ground maple, clover and other forage crops are repeated endlessly in big game cover.

Favorable game territory is easily pin-pointed, too, just from a study of land contours. In my big game book, *Art of Successful Deer Hunting*, a very careful evaluation was made of big game cover preferences in relation to warmth, food and shelter. It had been found that certain requirements touched off a lush growth, not only of big game browse, but a rich harvest of cones, nuts and berries made these "hot spots" boss for small game as well: squirrel, rabbit, grouse.

Primary requirement, of course, is warmth during the entire growing season. Warmth touches off a chain reaction which just naturally spells good hunting coverts. Territory receiving the longest period of sunshine, all during the growing season, is southern exposure—ridges, slopes and swales. These, which are high enough to receive proper "air drainage" always have a greater concentration of *all* wildlife.

Early spring sunshine pours on these southern exposures when snow is still clinging to the northern slopes. It carries through the golden months of autumn when maples are aflame along the hardwood ridges. There is not only a more abundant harvest of cones, nuts, wild grapes, berries and browse, but the food is also more favored by game because it is more nutritious.

A study of these natural concentrations is especially productive in connection with squirrel, rabbit or ruffed grouse hunting. It is a basic bit of sign reading which will take any hunting out of the luck category and place it on the more substantial basis of intelligent sign reading.

Just as surely as sign reading placed much of our shooting in front of us that day Art Richardson and I hunted ground squirrels and jacks, our stalking also made its contribution. A shot, be it at big game or small, is on the make from the time a hunter takes his first step until the game is in front of his rifle. Whether it will be an easy shot, or a difficult target to tag will depend in great part on the stalking which has gone before. Skillful stalking means easy, short range shooting. Unskillful stalking means poor, hurried chances for shots, difficult even for the most experienced and skilled rifle shot. Careful stalking is a basic technique of all good hunting from ground squirrels to deer or elk.

When I think of stalking and still hunting for either small game or large, I mentally see such splendid hunters as those seasoned woodsmen: Grant Hartwell, Elzie Randolph, Art Richardson, "Buck" Buoy easing through the cover, each step contributing something to that all important shot which they know is constantly on the make. Each of these hunters, trained to a fine point in the big and small game coverts by years of experience, move slowly. There is never a hasty, ill planned move in a day's hunt when they are afield. Slowness is basic. It is the very cornerstone on which successful hunting is built.

A predator stalking its quarry is methodically slow in its approach. It moves with stealth, getting within range. It takes every advantage the cover affords. Once, while hunting deer in a beautifully wooded south slope of a maple and hardwood forest, I was fortunate enough to witness the technique of a raccoon trying for a luscious, young ruffed grouse in a hazel thicket. It was late afternoon and I was easing along a deer trail. Stopping to con the cover ahead, my eyes were attracted by movement in the low growing hazel. I eased down on one knee to get a better view below heavy foliage and I saw this raccoon.

He was intent on something which I couldn't see from my position, so I eased forward on the trail a few feet and lay down flat, thus gaining a ringside seat to a bit of woodland drama.

The ruffed grouse walked back and forth, clucking and making small talk, but not unduly alarmed. It paused at times for a bit of leaf turning, though not entirely satisfied that all was on the up and up.

The raccoon moved belly low to the ground, slowly, carefully—always keeping a bush or clump of brush between it and its quarry. Not once did it make an unplanned move. Each time it eased forward some advantage accrued to this 'coon. He was certainly laying it on the line.

For minutes at a time he would remain perfectly motionless, his slender black fingers spread and gripping the ground, tensed for a spring if the agitated ruffed grouse quieted down and fed sufficiently close to make the pounce successful.

Here was a hunter who knew instinctively the importance of taking it slowly, or waiting it out, of keeping his hunt carefully in hand, ruling out everything except stealth.

I could hear my wristwatch ticking loudly. A maple leaf drifting down through the trees sounded dreadfully noisy. Time, however, apparently stood still for that black masked bandit. He was not hurrying his hunt, even though he must have tasted that tender young ruffed grouse while waiting a favorable opportunity to make the kill.

After fifteen minutes of careful stalking, in which he had moved twenty feet, he was directly behind a clump of hazel, with the ruffed grouse clucking and perting on the otherside —alerted, but not greatly alarmed. Then there was a flurry, a frantic beating of wings, feathers in the air—action so quick it could scarcely be followed, and the raccoon had his quarry.

It had been my intention to break it up before the climax of a kill, but I was so completely absorbed in the consummate job of stalking that the black hooded bandit was doing, I completely forgot. I moved along the trail again, intent on my own hunting, yet marveling at this nocturnal prowler who had gotten up early enough in the evening to get those nimble black fingers of his on a luscious supper. He certainly did not depend on luck.

Inexperienced hunters starting a day afield with ruffed grouse in mind, hunt haphazardly. They put their dogs down without knowing anything of cover preferences, of anything of the weather's effect on their hunting. Are those things only learned after years and years afield?

No! They are basic hunting requirements common to all game. Each time a hunter goes afield, regardless of his quarry, there is a dividend of basic hunting knowledge which has application when he changes from say squirrel to rabbit, from rabbit to ruffed grouse. The skill is transferable. Knowing that all hunting has basic requirements, and that each species hunted contributes something to over-all skill is sometimes harder to learn than the actual basic woodcraft envolved.

Al Lyman, a hunting partner, has a lazy old setter which he uses each autumn on ruffed grouse. The two make a splendid hunting combination. In twenty years of friendship I have never known Al to make an unnecessary move, either in or out of the game coverts. When he takes afield some warm October day with Indian summer touching the maples with mid-season warmth, he has all the time there is. Old abandoned apple orchards, with their crops of wormy apples will receive a slow, methodical visit from Al and his lazy old setter. So will the sun-warmed south slopes where the sugar ripe Oregon grapes still cling to the vines and the ridges where huckleberry bushes are covered with black shiny fruit.

Check off these ruffed grouse food preferences. They definitely add up to whitetail deer range. They add up to good squirrel hunting, too. You wouldn't go far wrong in such cover if you were out after cottontail rabbits with a couple of beagles, or just stillhunting bunnies with a .22 rifle. All would be hunting based on careful, fundamental evaluation—the sum total of all the tangibles which a hunter knows underlies all hunting.

Al Lyman, like all good hunters, regardless of quarry, breaks through the hard crust of luck to base his hunting on the more substantial foundation of good hunting technique. Even his slow, lazy old setter exemplified good hunting attitude by his slow methodical work.

Outstanding grouse dogs, of which there are very few, are slow and careful in their field work. They have a light touch which keeps game from flushing. And behind each ruffed grouse dog there is a truly great hunter—owner—a man fully conversant with basic hunting requirements.

All hunting, from small game to large, properly paced, is synchronized to the pulse of the game territory.

There are certain times of day when the woods and fields are active. Game is on the move, feeding, leaf turning, nut cutting on those warm slopes and draws where the rich wild harvest of food is produced each season. There are also periods when the coverts are quiet. Woodchucks are sunning themselves at the mouth of their dens. Ruffed grouse are dust bathing along the old tote roads. Squirrels are inactive, or at best doing little nut cutting or cornfield raiding. Deer have retired to sheltering thickets. It were as if nature slept away the drowsiness of midday, resting, waiting.

This inactive period starts late in the morning. It will last through until mid-afternoon for small game. It is a time when it is essential to match hunting technique to the mood of the quarry.

During an inactive period, any movement is much more attention getting and alarming. It will send a woodchuck scurrying for his hole, a ground squirrel to his burrow. The inactive period is a time of waiting out the hunt, of very careful stalking. You must be slow, slower yet, and alert beyond any casualness. For now you must see game at rest, a much more difficult undertaking than when there is movement to attract you.

Hurry and tenseness has no place in hunting in any event. Hunting is a time when all the senses must be alert and receptive. There must be a constant evaluation of cover, game habit, food preferences—a putting together of the jig-saw puzzle of the coverts.

Ever watch an experienced woodchuck hunter developing his hunt? Notice how he approaches the problem of making each segment fall in place, making it contribute some advantage to the over-all problem of stalking? There is no hurrying haphazardly across fields, hoping against hope that such hunting will turn up a few targets. He is constantly taking advantage of his cover, just as a still hunting deer hunter takes advantage of the deer coverts. An old stone fence leads the woodchuck hunter unobserved into a shooting position which will cover a clover field. A slight depression there gets him within range of a hillside pock-marked with woodhuck dens. Each bit of the hunt unfolds some advantage he can use in stalking. Basically it has much in common with a squirrel hunter in the hardwoods. There are elements of ruffed grouse hunting in it—the caution, the slowness, the constant evaluation of the cover. What a beautiful training ground it is for a hunter seriously using his small game hunting as a laboratory in which to develop big game hunting techniques!

No segment of a hunt stands out unrelated to the rest. The game you see, the ranges at which you must take your shots, are conditioned by the amount of skill you use in stalking—your hunting attitude. Hunting skill is not something primarily associated with wilderness, either. It is just as essential, and is as often found in a farm field or woodlot.

A soft stepping still hunter I know acquired his enviable deer stalking ability in a three acre woodlot hunting squirrel. Best snapshooting elk hunter I know acquired his rifle skill, and his careful stalking while hunting ground squirrel. I know a ruffed grouse hunter who has made six, one-shot kills on deer in heavy cover.

There has been a constant effort in the past to develop the "all-around rifle," one which would be suitable for game from woodchuck to elk. Preoccupation with this ideal has beclouded the issue of good hunting, placing the emphasis on the rifle, and not on the hunter where it belongs. It is much more to the point for a hunter to strive, not for the all around rifle, but instead for *all around hunting ability*. And that starts with basic hunting in the small game fields—the all around hunter.

CHAPTER 3

Sight Picture Is Not Enough

For accurate field shooting

When a ground squirrel or woodchuck sits up to consider the advisability of modestly retiring to his burrow, out there at an actual 200 yards, and an experienced hunter takes the shot with a .22/250, .243 Winchester, or some other excellent sniping caliber, he is seeing that target in reference to rifle performance and not in reference to actual 200 yards of range.

The fact of a 200 or 300 yard kill is always established after the shot, when the distance has been paced or otherwise measured.

The basic factors of accurate field shooting are sight picture and trigger squeeze. But alone they are not enough. The reason many excellent target range shots are not top performers in the game covers has been pondered by both the practical game shot and the very much more accurate target shot. Each time such enquiry is started, the investigation is centered about sight picture, trigger squeeze, the intangibles of woodcraft, with the probing for answers always stopping short of the actual cause of the discrepancy between range and field shooting.

When a skilled field shot snaps his rifle to shoulder, his sights reaching for a running fox squirrel scurrying along a high limb toward the security of his den, the hunter cheeks his rifle in a certain unchanging manner, but there is no sight picture in reference to his quarry. A *decision* must be made as to aiming point, and that will change with the target, the range, the time of day, to name just a few factors affecting uniformity of sight picture. There simply cannot be an unchanging target at an unchanging range in field shooting, with a rifleman getting the same sight picture each shot.

There is also a difference between the let-off of a good field shot and an equally good target shot. This difference becomes more pronounced as a hunter takes to the woods after squirrel, rabbit or other rifle targets, such as deer or elk. Open range woodchuck, sod poodles and crow shooting have much more in common with target positions, with the rifleman taking his shot from long range, using orthodox target stances for his shooting.

A field shot is conscious of let-off. He wills the shot at the most opportune instant, unlike the range shot who is taught to put increasing pressure on his trigger, the rifle being fired without the rifleman being conscious of the exact instant it will fire. But even here the good field shot must have more than a precise let-off for top performance.

That other, and all important factor in accurate field shooting is *range picture*. All skilled game shots, hunting anything from squirrel to moose, must have a range picture in reference to their rifle and target. This is the dividing line between good and mediocre field shooting.

Take a typical woodchuck shot. Perhaps the hunter cannot Indian up any closer than 200 yards, woodchucks being traditionally canny and dubious of a rifleman's intentions. The shot must be taken from here, or he will pop down his hole without a chance for the hunter to close the range. Let's say the rifle being used is a .243 Winchester, scoped with a nice 4X job.

Maybe, if this hunter is serious about developing small game skills which will pay off in the crimsoned autumn deer woods, he is using a big game scope—a flat topped post and cross hair, or maybe a Lee Dot reticle subtending two minutes of angle, more if the scope is of lesser power.

No one has measured those yards, mind you. No one will measure them until after the shot. Sure he may get a fairly accurate measure of distance by using his post or dot to cover the target, and by knowing something about the amount it subtends at different ranges, as well as the average size of his target. But, in reality, a hit or miss depends on the range picture.

Two hundred yards in hunting territory is a very flexible unit of measurement. Sometimes, under certain field conditions, it will stretch to unbelievable lengths. At other times this same yardage is short, incredibly short. It depends on the roughness of the terrain, your position, the position of the target—a hundred little factors which make each yard appear to be something other than three feet in length.

A well lighted target seems closer. A woodchuck in direct sunlight standing upright will seemingly shorten the range by at least fifty yards when compared to the same distance but with the quarry lying down in front of his den, or during an overcast period. Uphill targets appear closer than those seen downhill. Ranges across broken hill county appear longer than they really are. Level ground will shorten them to all appearances. Shots across a green clover field seem much longer than those obtained at the same distance across this field after the clover is cut, the stubble brown and shortened. Greens and blues in a landscape are associated with distance haze, and always spell out ranges longer than is actually the case.

See how many factors are militating against a hunter taking that woodchuck at 200 yards unless he had a good *range picture* for the *light* and *terrain* under which he must make the shot?

A .222 Remington Magnum, using a 55 grain bullet at a muzzle velocity of 3300 feet per second, sighted to hit point of aim 100 yards, is only 4 inches low at 200 yards, and 15 inches below point of aim at 300 yards. The .22/250, using the same 55 grain bullet, pushed at a velocity of 3800 feet a second, sighted to hit point of aim at 200 yards, is 1.1 inches high at 100 yards, and below point of aim by only 5.3 inches at 300 yards. Even with this fast stepping, flat shooting caliber, there is enough leeway for a clean miss at 300 yards, unless the range picture is understood.

Unless a hunter knows how lighting and terrain affect his range, reducing his conjectures to a matter of yards merely broaden the possibilities of error. Experienced field shots see it only as range picture. Subconsciously he is classifying this shot against previous ones. He is rejecting obvious mis-classifications. He is subconsciously remembering misses. It all adds up to a decision, not of so many precise yards, but of a comparison with another kill which gave this same range picture in regards to lighting, terrain and target.

You hear much about great instinctive game shots, not only with rifles but with shotguns as well. These individuals are supposed to be endowed with some esoteric sixth sense which gives them a skill we lesser hunters cannot hope to achieve in a lifetime of field shooting. But the only instinctive thing about their performance is their subconscious range pictures, derived from broad experience, which gives them hits under almost impossible gunning conditions.

A teal flaring across a duck blind, with a full gale behind him will be taken by only a great duck shot, one who has a range picture of the requirements of timing and lead necessary to hit that rocketing wind-sizzling duck.

It is only later that this hunter, and our man of the upland pastures with his .222 Remington Magnum tucked under his arm, when they are expansively promoting the idea that their respective shots were very skilled, which they were, that the idea of actual yardage creeps into the picture.

How does a hunter go about developing an instinctive sense for accurate range pictures in his field shooting? The small game field is the perfect laboratory, that and a specialized piece of equipment which will be considered after canvassing other factors of accurate field shooting.

But to get back to that woodchuck at a measured 200 yards—Suppose you detect him conning the sidehill from the security of his burrow, just his head and shoulders showing above the grass on a clouded day—a suggestion of thundershowers along the rim of the upland pasture hills. Specifically, you plan on blowing him up with a chest shot. But he is a much harder target to take, with all that non-vital area obscured by the tall sear grass, even though it is not your aiming point, regardless of the lighting. Why? Smallness and obscurity is subconsciously associated with distance. You must know these distracting factors for what they are to bring your range picture into focus, or you will subconsciously classify this as a much longer shot than it actually is. There will be an association with other and much longer shots.

If that woodchuck, after a careful culling of evidence, slips out into the short stubble, then again becomes suspicious and stands up for another conning of his immediate vicinity, and you can see him full length, you will revise that long range estimate. He no longer appears like that shot where you got a rock steady rest by placing your forearm on a granite boulder and took a woodchuck at what later proved to be 300 yards. That was the time you held the crosshairs about three inches above his head and got a hit in the chest area. Now, standing in the stubble, he appears like that shot you got across an upland pasture at an almost black chuck when it stood up at the mouth of its den, and you had a fair shot from a sitting position, resting your forearm across a stone wall.

One autumn, while hunting deer with Al Lyman, we eased along a ridge heavily forested with oak. Mast was thick on the ground, and several large bucks were fattening on the acorns. This particular day we managed to put the finger on a beautiful five pointer at about 80 yards. Al, kneeling to get a better view below the bough-line of intervening trees, could see his antlers and an ear, the head being turned sideways as our buck listened to some other hunter down hill. I suppose the target offered was about four inches in diameter. But the lighting was poor, the range picture slightly different.

I waited tensely, my eyes on a small opening which I hoped our quarry would cross if Al missed.

"Iffen I could see his shoulder, I could break his neck, easily," he whispered, "But I don't know, with just his head and horns showing."

After a moment which seemed like an hour, the buck took a cautious step forward, exposing his shoulder. Al's old .30/40 Krag slapped back against his shoulder, the echoes died away in the forest, but no deer crossed the small forest lane I watched.

We walked down through the thickets to our trophy. Al's bullet had clipped that buck behind the ear very neatly. There had been no hesitation in the shooting, no lack of confidence, once the game presented the proper range picture, or as Al put it later, when I questioned him, "When he looked normal to me."

Later, I was to remember that remark while hunting grey squirrel in the oak groves. And more and more, as I measured it by the yardstick of accurate field shooting, it made good common sense.

Those big greys were easily taken by head shots when they were sitting on a high oak limb. But let one begin to play it canny, watching me from his perch, with just his head showing, and the self same target was no longer an easy off-hand shot. A new element was projected into the setup. The range picture had changed to something unfamiliar, or at least not common to the type of shooting I normally did on squirrel.

The sight picture was still the same, for the aiming point in either case was the head. But until I had taken enough shots at squirrels just showing their heads to establish a norm, I wasn't as consistently accurate as when they exposed their entire body.

Just knowing that all these elements are projected into the setup will improve a hunter's field shooting.

When Art Richardson, my hunting friend, occasionally goes afield after jackrabbit or ground squirrel, leaving his .270 Winchester home, and taking his old .38/40 lever action, there is method in his madness. This rifle, with its rainbow trajectory curve makes him acutely conscious of all the elements of accurate field shooting. Distances are emphasized, not in yards, but in effective ranges.

Up to a certain point, trajectory cancels out range. A flat shooting varmint rifle such as the .270 using a 100 grain bullet, the .22/250 or the .222 Remington Magnum with a 55 grain bullet, can put a field shot on the right side of the ledger. But still, even with these fast stepping calibers, the skilled field shot either consciously or subconsciously has a range picture when he touches one off.

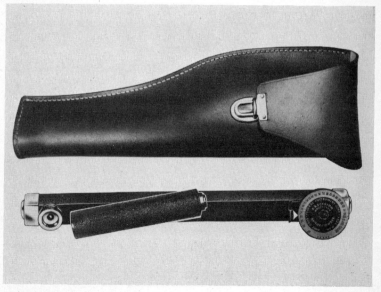

Federal rangefinder. Accurate to a plus or minus of about 3%. Use of a rangefinder is not only an excellent way of measuring ranges, but also leads to more accurate estimates when the ranges are estimated without its use.

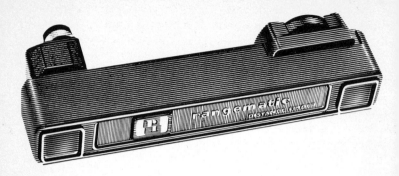

The Rangematic rangefinder. It has an insert chart giving the bullet path above and below line of sight. In use, insert the proper range chart to find bullet drop beyond point of aim. Example: .30/06 150-grain bullet, 3,000 fps, sighted to hit point of aim at 200 yards—the chart will show exactly how much drop one must contend with for a long range shot beyond the sighting distance (9¾ inch drop at 300 yards, 16¾ inches at 350 yards) all the way out to 500 yards by 50-yard increments where the bullet drop is 50¾ inches. The instrument comes with carrying case.

Recently I tested two different range finders that prove excellent for measuring ranges on the rough terrain of the small game hunter. These two ranges finders, one manufactured by The Federal Instrument Company, the other by Ranging Inc., were both very accurate under field shooting conditions. Either of these instruments will teach a hunter more about the light effect on field ranges, rough terrain, etc. than anything that I have examined. These range finders are accurate to a plus or minus of 4 percent out to 500 yards with the longer range models. They certainly are to be recommended for the small game hunter who is using the small game fields to develop his big game hunting techniques.

There should be no slavish dependence on a range finder before you have formed your own opinion of the range. Rather it should be used to check your own *range pictures.* Used in this manner, it certainly will save you a lot of weary pacing off of long shots, of trying to find out the reason for unaccountable misses when the sights were right, the let-off perfect, and no wind to harry your light, fast stepping bullet.

No question about range picture, once you have used a range finder to check a shot. Maybe it is paradoxical to say that by using a range finder to give you precise measurements in yards, it will train you to see your ranges, not as a measurement reduced to yards, but as range pictures giving you maximum field shooting accuracy, but it is fact. Range pictures, to an experienced field shot are as precise and as attention getting as the crosshairs centered on a grey or fox squirrel or a woodchuck taking a sunbath in front of his den. They are basic factors of all accurate field shooting and have very, very little to do with estimates of range in actual yards.

CHAPTER 4

Small Game Field Shooting Positions

The trail lead through a frost-touched multicolored forest, the oak and maple trees a riot of crimsons, deep reds and browns. A golden autumn haze filled the valleys, and if you listened you could hear quail calling lonesomely for the lost summer. Grant Hartwell and I were walking this ridge trail, as men should be doing each autumn, our minds on deer, light overnight packs on our backs, wholly content with the world.

While deer was the prime objective, a couple of grey squirrels for a stew wouldn't be amiss, nor for that matter a blue grouse.

Swinging around a bend we flushed a big old buster of a blue grouse. It angled up through the trees with a frantic beating of wings and perched on an oak limb about thirty yards away, neck outstretched, its nervousness reflected in its constant stepping about as it watched our every move. We remained perfectly quiet for a space of a few moments, knowing that the least untoward movement would touch off our hair triggered game at once. When it quieted down a bit, Grant eased over a few steps toward the huge mossy bole of an oak, rested his forearm against it for the shot.

I waited intently, my pulse surging just as strongly as if he had a big buck under his sights. The silence was shattered by the roar of his .30/30 Model 99 Savage. The grouse tumbled from its lofty perch into the deep mast under the trees, drummed frantically for a moment then lay still. I walked over and picked up our quarry. Its head had been neatly severed by that 170 grain slug, an excellent bit of small game field shooting.

Small game field shooting has problems of positions which merit a lot of study and practice by hunters. Fortunately there is no essential difference between small and large game shooting, and what is learned in the small game fields is directly applicable to big game coverts. Each places emphasis on the time element, practical accuracy and range picture.

Quite often the decision as to shooting position is made by the game itself. A squirrel alerted by your careful stalking, waiting for a tip-off from you before taking to the security of its den tree, has so compressed the time element you have in which to get off the shot, you must take it from the position in which you find yourself, more often than not a snapshot off-hand.

When Art Richardson and I were hunting ground squirrel that early June morning, taking them "field run," each shot was governed by the game itself, to a great extent. Squirrels scurrying toward the protection of their burrows had snap-shooting written all over them. Those which stood up momentarily to inspect their surroundings had the same urgency in their attitude.

Essentially, there are three basic field shooting positions which are practical, and used for more than ninety-eight per cent of all field shooting. These three positions are: standing, sitting and kneeling. The prone position can sometimes also be used in long range woodchuck sniping and in mountain hunting. But a too slavish use of the prone position tends to a deliberateness wholly at odds with field accuracy because of the time element usually interjected by the game itself.

Modifications of the three prime field shooting positions: sitting, standing and kneeling, are almost infinite in number.

Game, large or small, are either in motion or have the threat of movement. The times you will find game at rest, with no threat of explosive action are comparatively rare. Usually it is movement which first attracts a hunter, and that not only conditions field shooting positions but also the shot itself.

Offhand shooting requires the most skill, and is the most used in field shooting, and at the same time it is one in which most hunters are least competent. There is an obvious modification of range technique in offhand field shooting. An offhand field shot is precise and clear cut in action—no hesitation—when the sights are on, the shot is made immediately. Trigger squeeze and sight alignment complement each other, each an integral part of practical field accuracy.

Offhand snapshooting stance is more readily learned from shooting than from the rifle range.

Next a careful synchronizing of trigger squeeze and sight alignment, balance is important in offhand field shooting. Misses in this type field shooting can very often be traced to an off balanced position. When any game flushes wildly, squirrel, deer, elk or rabbit, and the gunner is caught off-balance, his ability to get on the target, to lead his quarry when necessary, is so greatly complicated that a vital hit is almost an impossibility.

Balance stripped of its esoteric nonsense, means simply that you are on your two good feet, ready to step forward or back to give you the most stable position for your shot. And that simmers down to bringing your feet close enough together so you can swivel from the hips to follow your game without the compelling necessity of shuffling around, once your rifle is at your shoulder.

On running shots a hunter is swinging with his game as his rifle comes up. The instant the butt of his rifle touches his shoulders, his sights are on. For he has done the basic sighting as his rifle is mounted. It comes up aligned for a snapshot.

Al Lyman, easing along a hardwood ridge, his rifle at the carry, can explode into action with a smoothness and deadly precision which is the hallmark of all great field shots. Deer, elk, grey squirrel, rabbit, no matter the game, there is no hesitation, no groping for the best position from which to take the shot. "Iffen I get my feet 'pinted' right, the rest is easy," he once told me. Getting one's feet pointed right for an off-hand snapshot is not as far fetched as it seems, either. If you are a right handed rifleman, and go into action with your left foot pointed directly at the position where your game is flushing, initial alignment has been accomplished. Not only that, but you are now in a position to keep your target under your sights through a 180 degree circle without moving your feet, swiveling from the hips to follow your game. In order to do this, your feet cannot be more than fourteen inches apart, or you will find your position becoming more cramped on the follow through.

In assuming the offhand field shooting position, your

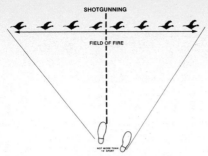

SHOTGUNNING

FIELD OF FIRE

NOT MORE THAN 12 APART

(Right-handed gunner) His left foot points toward the center of the field of fire. Squared to the target as illustrated here, there is no lockup in body movement and a smooth swing is possible for a bird in any part of the field of fire, the gunner swiveling from the hips. Weight shifts slightly from right to left foot for a bird in the left portion of the field of fire, going from right to left. This is reversed for a bird going from left to right, when weight is shifted slightly to the right foot.

weight is on the balls of your feet. Your body leans slightly forward, arm extended well out on the forearm of your rifle, relaxed and free swinging. Maybe you will actually follow your target with your rifle; more often you will swing ahead to a small opening, intercepting your game at a point which affords the only clear shooting.

It takes practice to develop form, but form underlies all field shooting skills. Small game hunting is an ideal place in which to iron out inaccuracies, not only because the same type shots are called for here as you will later use in big game hunting, but also because you have a much more extended season, so many more chances to improve your skill.

Snapshooting is one phase of offhand shooting. There are other phases of almost equal importance, especially squirrel hunting with a rifle. Quite often it is possible to get additional steadiness for a precise shot by resting an arm against the side of a tree, log, or rock ledge—easing off the shot from a standing position with the steadiness of a kneeling or sitting stance.

Any rifle, however, more powerful than a .22 rimfire will tend to "shoot away" from a rest. Where the rifle itself is held directly against the side of a tree, and the shot taken at 100 yards or so, this tendency can make a mighty contribution toward a miss, especially if the target is fairly small. Some rifles will move their point of impact as much as four or five inches

Offhand shooting position. On running shots at deer there is an element of shotgun shooting in the routine. No time for a sling—no nothin' except a fast, accurate shot. If you have trouble with the offhand position in deer hunting then this should be the position to use in all your small game shooting, stalking within medium range for the shots. Note flexibility of the foot positions—steady without strain.

to one side when thus held. The same condition exists, when a rifle is placed across a rock or log for the shot, except now it will shoot high. All rifles should be cushioned with a hand between it and any steadying rest, regardless of the position used.

Sitting position is best for those intermediate shots at small game such as woodchuck, ground squirrel, coyote or other predator far enough away that careful stalking hasn't alarmed it. In a sitting position, the body acts as a tripod support for your rifle, giving a very steady stance from which to make a precision shot. Properly positioned, you are turned well away from your intended target, feet well apart, elbows resting on, or slightly over, the knees. However, some very good field shots cross their feet, and one excellent game shot never rests his trigger arm on his knee at all, maintaining that a follow up shot is much faster with his lever action when he doesn't have to disturb his shooting stance by going out of position, as it were, to reload.

While sitting is an excellent small game shooting position, it, like the offhand position, has the added virtue of being frequently used in big game hunting. Any skill developed in small game and pest shooting using this position, is directly aimed at improving your big game shooting accuracy. My field notes indicate that while hunting mule deer in the comparatively open ranges of the West I have used the sitting position for at least half of the shots obtained, and for all shots except those taken in the jackpine thickets and other heavily forested areas. In these, of course, it was a case of snapshooting.

The sitting position is an easy one in which to drop for a shot calling for additional steadiness. But it does require practice to develop the necessary skill to make it effective afield. That means practice out in the small game field, where the ground is uneven, and the game places a premium on time. It is well to try a few "dry runs" in this position when you are afield, even before trying for a small game or pest shot. It is an excellent way of ironing out rough spots in one's technique.

Kneeling has many more field shooting virtues than one would at once suppose. It is not as steady as the sitting position, but is much faster. Its chief virtue is that it gives you a comparatively unobstructed view for a shot in a forest by placing you below the bough line of the trees.

Once while hunting snowshoe rabbit in jackpine thickets, I obtained four shots at these oversized bunnies, and in each instance I had to take them from the kneeling position to get below the snow laden limbs of the trees. In this same section, only a few days later, I managed to finagle a big buck by using the kneeling position.

There are probably more excellent prone rifle shots than riflemen with any great degree of competence in any of the other positions. By the same token, the prone position has fewer hunting virtues than any other field position. But if its negative qualities stopped here, it wouldn't be so bad. Unfortunately, however, prone shooting robs riflemen of confidence in the more practical offhand, sitting and kneeling positions.

Kneeling position with a rifle, sling not in use. Note how left elbow is steadied on the knee.

When the target is a fox squirrel in the top of a butternut or a grey squirrel playing it canny in an oak with a breeze ruffling the leaves and the target unsteady, then the shot must be taken from a standing position, and prone rifle practice can contribute nothing to the skill required for a killing shot.

There is, however, one virtue retrievable from prone rifle shooting. Quite often a hunter has a chance to lie across a rock, stump or other object for a shot. While technically I suppose this could scarcely be called prone rifle shooting, it does give rock steadiness for a shot, and in addition it gives a fair view above fern, grass and other low growing stuff which would prevent a hunter from taking the shot lying directly on the ground.

Each field shooting position has a different yardstick of accuracy by which to measure its effectiveness. Each position is a compromise.

In offhand snapshooting a hunter trades *accuracy for time.* Offhand targets, such as a squirrel scurrying for its den tree or a woodchuck streaking through the clover stubble, has a time element built into the shot which cancels out the more accurate shooting positions, such as sitting or kneeling. But if the range is short, a hunter can swap the additional accuracy of a sitting position for the extra split seconds of a snapshot. If he does score a miss with his first shot, he is still in position for another following shot.

When ranges are extended and the game is unalarmed, the reverse is true. A hunter can trade time for additional accuracy.

Once, while coming out of the wilderness section of the Pistol River section of southwestern Oregon, after a small game hunting-fishing expedition, I waited while Hartwell made a very careful stalk of a grey squirrel. This was the last day of our trip, and camp grub consisted of about a cup of flour, some salt and pepper, a smear of lard—enough to cook a squirrel.

I could see a trade coming up as Grant eased toward a large oak. When he came alongside this tree, he waited for

Trying for a head shot in squirrel hunting with a .22 Marlin Model 39 lever-action. Scope is a 2.5X with medium crosshairs. Note that rifle doesn't touch the tree, but rests on the author's left hand.

the squirrel to sit up with an acorn, affording a nice target. Grant, apparently, was going to trade the fast shooting qualities of an offhand effort for a more accurate shot from a rest. I watched him place his gun arm along side the lichen covered bole of the oak for his shot, pause, then fire.

At the shot our quarry came tumbling down, to lie in the mast, a nice plump grey for our midday meal.

The shot was made with a handgun, a subject covered in a separate chapter, but the episode thoroughly exemplifies the compromise inherent in all field shooting positions. Each shot, even at the expense of reiteration, is a definite compromise between ultimate speed and ultimate accuracy. Split second decisions are built into each shooting opportunity afield. How well you weigh speed of the different field positions against their accuracy, in a large measure, determines their effectiveness.

PART II

Small Game
Hunting Rifles

CHAPTER 5

Small Game And Varmint Rifles

The center-fires

At first glance the problem of selecting a small game and varmint rifle would appear a relatively simple undertaking. A hunter has clean killing in mind, which means hair splitting accuracy and fair ranging qualities.

Hunting rifle weight must be a good compromise for steady holding and portability, say eight to nine pounds, for a field rifle is carried much more than it is shot.

All these requirements are easily met, yet the selection must be approached with caution. Many hunting skills hinge on the type of rifle taken afield. For example, short range rifles are very apt to be owned by excellent still hunters and stalkers, long range rifles by precision field shots. When a rifle is selected which has both qualities, you have an unbeatable combination on the make—the all-around hunter and field shot. But the selection is no push-over.

Maybe it is best to break down the problem of rifle selection into two categories for detailed study, even though the basic thing which should be studied is *trends* in small game center-fire calibers. Small game rifles are of two classes, wildcats and standard factory calibers.

Let's start with the wildcats. Experiment is the very life blood of progress, and modern day hunters owe a lot to the wildcat experimenter who was never quite satisfied with the performance of available rifles. While some of their products were off-beat from start to finish, they explored many blind alleys in their search for longer range and greater accuracy.

The wildest of the wildcats are plenty wild indeed! All in all, however, many worthwhile improvements came from theory and experimentation. Results of these experiments are constantly being passed back to us lesser hunters in the form of better accuracy, ranging and killing ability.

Something else has also been passed along which is not on the right side of the ledger: a lot of misrepresentation about velocities and accuracy. An outdoorsman looking for a rifle with which to finagle a woodchuck in an upland pasture some early spring day, when the clover is first tarnishing the brown winter stubble with green, the dogwood is starting to bloom along the old stone fences, goes afield with a very poor wildcat rifle selection—all because he didn't investigate carefully before selecting his small game rifle.

A 48 grain .22 caliber bullet can be driven close to 4500 feet a second in some of these privately designed rifles. That is a lot of velocity, but a rifleman gets it by paying for it with shortened barrel life, and in many calibers at the expense of hair splitting sniper accuracy.

Two requirements of woodchuck sniping have sent experimenters along the path of high velocity: a desire for bullet breakup on impact, and a nipping off of bullet drop over extended field ranges.

In settled farm communities it is essential for a varmint bullet to breakup completely when it hits the earth, otherwise you will have a ricochet buzzing like an angry bee out across the meadows, something not conducive to either safety or good farmer-sportsman relationship. To prevent ricocheting, velocities must not fall much below 2400 feet per second. Fortunately, this problem has been well licked in all the modern wildcat calibers, as well as in the factory calibers designed for long range small game sniping.

How about bullet drop over the longer ranges? Just to show how far we have come in licking this problem, let's take a look at one of today's calibers.

.243 WINCHESTER BULLET PATH ABOVE OR BELOW LINE OF SIGHT AT:
(80 gr. bullet, 3500 f.p.s., sighted in to be dead on at 200 yards)

50 yards	100 yards	200 yards	250 yards	400 yards
−0.2″	+1.1 inch above	0	5⅛″ inches below	−17″

While the .243 Winchester isn't the highest velocity rifle available for small game hunting, it does have the merit of being a very good deer caliber, using the .243 100 grain bullet at a muzzle velocity of about 3100 feet a second.

Broken down into effective field shooting ranges it becomes obvious that rifles of the .243 Winchester class have an advantage of about 150 yards range on small game and pest targets. In addition, and as an added merit, it will shoot close to one minute of angle for accuracy, producing three inch groups or less at 300 yards.

Out to three hundred fifty yards, bullet breakup on impact is excellent with all modern small game calibers delivering a muzzle velocity of 3,000 to 3,500 feet a second.

It goes without saying that most small game snipers are reloaders, producing ammunition equal if not superior to factory ammunition. This being the case, there is little handicap in owning a wildcat caliber, provided it is adapted to factory bullets.

Factory calibers, such as the .222 Remington, .243 Winchester, and a host of other calibers have been "improved" by rifle experimenters—wildcatting being an off-season sport with them. This improving is done by reaming standard rifle chamber to give a straighter taper and a more abrupt shoulder. In some calibers these "improvements" have produced better accuracy and higher velocity without increasing pressures beyond a safe margin. In others, results have been more apparent in the writings of rifle partisans for the specialized caliber than in the field testing.

Small game hunters should remember that in going for one of these improved chambering jobs, unless the improved chamber will accept factory ammunition, and the "improvement" is brought about by fireforming the cases, he is letting himself in for considerable trouble in resizing brass for his sniping rifle.

Improved versions are best when they are along the lines of the Ackley .257 and the Weatherby .257 Magnum, either of which will handle factory ammunition.

The trouble of resizing brass for a wildcat caliber, however, is sometimes well worth the effort. The .22/250 Varminter cartridge is made by necking down the .250/3000 case. The .25/06 requires resizing. Both are exceptional wildcat calibers. They are two of perhaps a half dozen wildcats which are destined to become better known over the years. There are many other calibers requiring manual resizing of brass with few field shooting virtues to recommend them.

Do plenty of sign reading before laying your iron men on the line for a wildcat.

Those which have enough virtues to be taken up by an increasing number of hunters each year all have one thing in common, regardless of caliber. Powder capacity of case, bullet weight and caliber, either through careful experiment or happy accident, are all *in balance*. There seems to be no critical bullet weight, velocity or powder charge. Case design and capacity give each caliber a flexibility which makes for hair splitting accuracy with a wide range of loadings.

A balanced load, such as the .22/250 Varminter has so many intangibles in its makeup even the most advanced experimenters cannot place their fingers on *all* the factors. It is known that cases of medium capacity with only a medium powder charge often give higher velocity and better accuracy than larger size cases using heavier charges of powder.

Overlarge cartridge capacity in reference to bullet weight often gives high pressure readings without a corresponding increase in velocity. And when they are accurate, it is usually with one particular loading. The flexibility apparent in those balanced calibers is lacking. A rifleman using one for his sniping has a headache from start to finish. Flexibility in small game rifles is important. It is much more so in the rifleman himself. Just about any caliber will serve in the hands of a competent rifleman able to bring out its full ranging and killing potential.

Last July, while walking across my upland pastures, I came upon Al Lyman behind a red cedar tree. He was peering intently across a small draw. Seeing me, he motioned me down, then signaled me up to where he was lying. Inching my way to his position I studied the hillside where midsummer had begun to tan the grass and burnish the greasewood with a swarthy Indian hue. I saw the object of his concern, a ground squirrel fooling around the base of a stump, eating dandelions.

Eventually it worked its way out into the opening, sat up and gave the hillside a careful searching before committing itself to any more foraging which might lead it any farther from the security of its burrow. Al eased up his rifle, steadied it, and at the report that squirrel dropped. Range? About 150 yards. Rifle? A Model 64 Winchester, using a handload of 27 grains of Du Pont 3031 powder, a 100 grain jacketed softpoint bullet. It was my handloading, as a matter of fact, and my rifle. Al Lyman had borrowed it as he came by the ranch house.

We talked awhile before I left him to continue my walk across the pastures, after being cautioned not to cross certain hillsides he planned to hunt. "Put down them digger squirrels," he explained, a breach of hunting ethics even landowners should not commit. "Furthermore, you might tell Ethel to hold up dinner until about two o'clock. Won't get my diggering done before then. They have been barking all over the hillsides." So advised and cautioned, I left him.

That rifle he was using was certainly a long ways down the list from some of the super duper wildcats. It did exemplify one thing, however. Rifles of very modest velocities and killing power can be used for *all* small game and pest shooting. (Remember Art Richardson and that old .38/40 Winchester hunting jack rabbits and ground squirrels, Chapter I?)

My .25/35 Model 64, equipped with a Redfield Sourdough front sight and a Williams Foolproof receiver sight, has enough accuracy and enough ranging ability to make it an interesting sniping rifle in anybody's pastures. Of course precautions must be taken to see that all field targets have suitable background so there will not be ricochet.

Small game hunters are probably better served by selecting factory calibers. You can handload for them, and in addition use factory loads to obtain the necessary brass for developing just the right loading for any gunning situation you have. The .222 Remington is an excellent choice, especially in the Sako Mauser action, as exemplified by the Marlin Model 322. This rifle is built by the Marlin Firearms Company, using their Micro-Groove rifling, a shallow sixteen groove rifling which gives very little bullet deformation, and a consequent increase in accuracy of about twenty per cent over conventional deep, six groove rifling.

Another very good factory caliber is the .243 Winchester. It is strictly an out-an-out long range varmint rifle, though at first appearance in the game fields, a lot of extravagant claims were made for its ability as a big game elk shooting caliber.

The .257 Roberts started out as a wildcat, but it has been a standard factory caliber for several decades. It is very accurate with all three factory loadings: 117 grain, 100 grain and 87 grain bullets. Best accuracy, though, is with the two heavier weight loadings. The 117 grain bullet makes an excellent varmint loading especially in the mountainous areas where there are apt to be constant thermal winds. Due to its good sectional density, there is much less drift with this bullet than there is with many of the lighter, higher speed ones.

For a hunter who cannot afford more than one rifle, the .257 Roberts, either standard or in Ackley's improved chambering, would be an excellent all around choice. It is a nice deer caliber with its heavier loadings. For hunting tree squirrel or rabbit it can be midranged with handloads to about the velocity of a .22 long rifle.

The 250/3000 Savage is a superbly accurate sniping rifle. A small game hunter with a liking for a lever action would find this an excellent choice. Factory loading gives the 87 grain bullet 3000 feet a second. In addition a 100 grain bullet can be driven 2820 feet a second. By careful handloading this caliber will duplicate the velocities of practically all calibers from the .22 long rifle to the .25/20, giving it a versatility in the small game field which makes it truly an all-around caliber.

Another lever action .25 caliber which must be considered is the before mentioned but now obsolete .25/35. How badly handicapped would a hunter be, armed with a .25/35 Winchester Model 64 lever action? Let's look at some of the adverse factors which can be ironed out. First is the fact that all tubular magazine rifles are not supposed to use Spitzer pointed bullets. It doesn't come under the head of pleasure to have a pointed bullet tickling the primer of the cartridge in front of it in a tubular magazine rifle. But Spitzer pointed bullets can be used in tubular magazine rifles just the same. It reduces magazine capacity to exactly one cartridge, and with one in the chamber, makes it a two shot repeater.

Snapshooting at running targets, acquiring skill for those big game covers, this limited magazine capacity has some advantages. Emphasis is placed on individual shots, much more so than if a hunter has a full magazine to unload on his target.

As for ranging ability, 200 yards will cover most small game and varmint ranges, and the .25/35, with handloads, is sufficiently accurate to kill consistently at this range. On the heavier pests, such as coyotes, the 117 grain bullet is an excellent killer, with plenty of penetration to drive through from any quarter to reach the vital area. Ranges beyond 200 yards, when one is using a comparatively short range sniping rifle, are problems of stalking, an ability which always pays off later in big game hunting. All in all, the small game hunter using a .25/35 wouldn't be greatly handicapped for most off-season hunting.

Present-day lever-action fanciers, using such rifles as the Model 99 Savage and the Winchester Model 88 are not troubled with tubular magazines that prevented the use of pointed bullets. These rifles, with box or rotary magazines, are adapted to the most modern bullets. The factory calibers such as the .243 Winchester in the Model 88 or the same caliber in the Savage Model 99 are excellent all-around small game rifles. Both can be reloaded to reduced velocities for out and out squirrel hunting in the hardwoods. Both are excellent for longer range, more open shooting.

The .222 Remington is never a mistake for small game and pest shooting. It hasn't the wind bucking ability of some of the heavier calibers, nor their ranging qualities, but within that critical 200 yard range it is highly accurate. It can be handloaded down to a velocity of 1400 hundred feet using a 43 grain gas check bullet and 3.5 grains of Unique Pistol powder. The .22 Remington Magnum, an "improved" version of the standard factory caliber will drive its bullets at a full 3200 feet a second. It is the better selection for small game shooters interested in handloading. It will not only give high velocities with maximum charges, but all the midrange loads work out well.

When one takes a .270 down from the gunrack, it is quite possible that, measured from the standpoint of all around versatility, it is the best sniping rifle of the lot. It will reach out with the wildest of the wildcats. It will make groups as small. In addition, it is a good caliber on larger game, such as black bear and deer, with proper loads. Some hunters endorse it as an elk rifle, but I cannot string along on this—just not enough lead, even with the best handloads and heaviest bullets it will handle.

But for the one rifle man the .270 has many advantages over the .250/3000, or the .257. And of course, when it comes to a comparison with such short range lead slingers as the other rifles under consideration, there just isn't any contest—if your choice is a bolt action a .270, 100 grain bullet can be driven at 3500 feet a second. The 130 grain factory load is given a velocity of 3140 feet a second—both are superbly accurate.

Using the 100 grain bullet at a velocity of 3500 feet a second, a .270 sighted in to hit point of aim at 200 yards is very effective on woodchuck and other targets to a full 300 yards. That is something to ponder when one is tempted by a flat shooting wildcat. What a surprise it would be to a coyote lurking out around the 300 yard mark! Those sly predators seem to have the range of lesser calibers gauged to a nicety, but a .270 could give them cause for reappraisal.

A very versatile small game caliber is none other than the old reliable .30/06! Sure it is loud-mouthed, and not the best for settled farm country. But there is still a whale of a lot of small game and varmint territory where this old proven caliber is ideal. I know it is smart to consider it more or less a has been. But remember, more experimenting has been done with .30/06 loadings than any other caliber. More loading data have accumulated over the years in all velocity brackets and bullet weights than for any other rifle. There are extant over three hundred different handloads developed by riflemen using this caliber during the past several decades. Just about all types of field shooting and game have been considered by some rifleman-hunter and a .30/06 load developed for it.

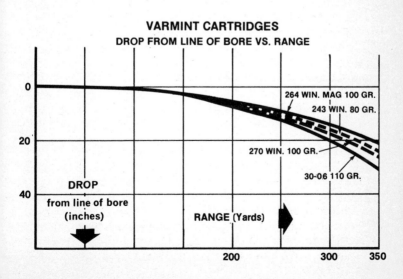

VARMINT CARTRIDGES
DROP FROM LINE OF BORE VS. RANGE

Want a good midrange load, something with about the velocity of a .22 long rifle for tree squirrels and cottontails? You have been anticipated by other .30/06 riflemen. A 153 grain gas check bullet driven by 12 grains of Du Pont 4759 will give you a velocity of 1100 feet a second. That would make a nice pot hunting load on a big game trip. It would also be a good load for practice shooting where range facilities are limited.

Maybe, though, you have woodchuck or ground squirrel in mind. A 110 grain jacketed bullet can be driven at 3270 feet a second with 54.5 grains of Dupont IMR. 4895. Of course a 110 grain, .30 caliber bullet hasn't the best sectional density for sustained velocities over extended ranges, but it has good accuracy and breakup out to 200 yards, and that is a lot of range in anybody's hunting territory.

This listing of rifles for small game hunting is incomplete. This is more a pointing out of trends in calibers and loadings which the small game hunter and varmint sniper might consider in selecting his equipment with big game hunting as the ultimate consideration. I often use my .348 with reduced loads for tree squirrel, finding it superbly accurate for this type hunting. I often use it on ground squirrel with a 150 grain bullet driven at 2835 feet per second with a charge of 58.5 grains of Du Pont 4064. All this off-season shooting adds up to clean kills on the deer and elk trails.

In selecting a small game rifle, you should canvass thoroughly the type of hunting you will do, both in the small game field and later in the big game coverts.

All my rifles, from .22 rimfires to my heaviest caliber are practical stalking rifles—hunter sighted. Occasionally I like to pick up a rifle which is utterly strange to me, and go hunting, such as that .22 Mossberg I used diggering (Chapter 1). But for the most part I find it much more to the point to keep sights, trigger pulls, actions and weights very closely duplicated from small game rifles to large.

The build up of shooting habits—the confidence which comes of using familiar materials has something of a craftsman's or artist's desire for complete mastery of his medium. A rifleman feels the same thrill from proper mastery of *his* materials, and the same sense of achievement. When a shot is delivered at the end of a careful stalk which has brought out the best in woodcraft of which the rifleman is capable, and accuracy is crowned with a clean kill, that, it seems to me, is the ultimate in hunting satisfaction. And it starts with rifle selection, too.

Selecting a rifle is primarily a matching of that rifle to the hunter, a secondary matching to the game on which it will be used. After this careful matching of *center-fire* rifles, there is still a rifle problem to be answered. What type .22 rimfire should I use, a heavy target rifle, bolt action, single shot, lever action?

Center-fire Rifle Cartridges

Cartridge	Wt. Grs.	Bullet Type	Velocity (fps)				Energy (ft. lbs.)				Mid-Range Trajectory (inches)		
			Muzzle	100 yds.	200 yds.	300 yds.	Muzzle	100 yds.	200 yds.	300 yds.	100 yds.	200 yds.	300 yds.
218 Bee Super-X and Super-Speed	46	OPE(HP)	2860	2160	1610	1200	835	475	265	145	0.7	3.8	11.5
22 Hornet Super-X and Super-Speed	45	SP	2690	2030	1510	1150	720	410	230	130	0.8	4.3	13.0
22 Hornet Super-X and Super-Speed	46	OPE(HP)	2690	2030	1510	1150	740	420	235	135	0.8	4.3	13.0
22-250 Super-X and Super-Speed	55	PSP	3810	3270	2770	2320	1770	1300	935	655	0.3	1.6	4.4
220 Swift Super-X and Super-Speed	48	PSP	4110	3490	2930	2440	1800	1300	915	635	0.3	1.4	3.8
222 Remington Super-X and Super-Speed	50	PSP	3200	2660	2170	1750	1140	785	520	340	0.5	2.5	7.0
225 Winchester Super-X and Super-Speed	55	PSP	3650	3140	2680	2270	1630	1200	875	630	0.4	1.8	4.8
243 Winchester (6mm) Super-X and Super-Speed	80	PSP	3500	3080	2720	2410	2180	1690	1320	1030	0.4	1.8	4.7
243 Winchester (6mm) Super-X and Super-Speed	100	PP(SP)	3070	2790	2540	2320	2090	1730	1430	1190	0.5	2.2	5.5
25-06 Super-X and Super-Speed	90	PEP	3500	3090	2730	2420	2450	1910	1490	1170	0.4	1.8	4.7
25-06 Super-X and Super-Speed	120	PEP	3120	2850	2600	2360	2590	2160	1800	1480	0.5	2.0	5.5
25-20 Winchester	86	L, Lead	1460	1180	1030	940	405	265	200	170	2.6	12.5	32.0
25-20 Winchester	86	SP	1460	1180	1030	940	405	265	200	170	2.6	12.5	32.0
25-35 Winchester Super-X and Super-Speed	117	SP	2300	1910	1600	1340	1370	945	665	465	1.0	4.6	12.5
250 Savage Super-X and Super-Speed	87	PSP	3030	2660	2330	2060	1770	1370	1050	820	0.6	2.5	6.4
250 Savage Super-X and Super-Speed	100	ST(Exp)	2820	2460	2140	1870	1760	1340	1020	775	0.6	2.9	7.4
*256 Winchester Magnum Super-X	60	OPE	2800	2070	1570	1220	1040	570	330	200	0.8	4.0	12.0
257 Roberts Super-X and Super-Speed	87	PSP	3200	2820	2460	2150	1980	1530	1170	890	0.5	2.2	5.7
257 Roberts Super-X and Super-Speed	100	ST(Exp)	2900	2540	2210	1920	1870	1430	1080	820	0.6	2.7	7.0
*257 Roberts Super-X	100	PP(SP)	2900	2540	2210	1920	1870	1430	1080	820	0.6	2.7	7.0
*257 Roberts Super-X	117	PP(SP)	2650	2280	1950	1690	1824	1350	985	740	0.7	3.4	8.8
264 Winchester Magnum Super-X and Super-Speed	100	PSP	3700	3260	2880	2550	3040	2360	1840	1440	0.4	1.6	4.2
264 Winchester Magnum Super-X and Super-Speed	140	PP(SP)	3200	2940	2700	2480	3180	2690	2270	1910	0.5	2.0	4.8
270 Winchester Super-X and Super-Speed	100	PSP	3480	3070	2690	2340	2690	2090	1600	1215	0.5	2.1	5.3
270 Winchester Super-X and Super-Speed	130	PP(SP)	3140	2880	2630	2400	2847	2390	2000	1660	0.5	2.1	5.3
270 Winchester Super-X and Super-Speed	130	ST(Exp)	3140	2850	2580	2320	2847	2340	1920	1550	0.5	2.1	5.3
270 Winchester Super-X and Super-Speed	150	PP(SP)	2900	2620	2380	2160	2802	2290	1890	1550	0.6	2.5	6.3
284 Winchester Super-X and Super-Speed	125	PP(SP)	3200	2880	2590	2310	2843	2300	1860	1480	0.5	2.1	5.3
284 Winchester Super-X and Super-Speed	150	PP(SP)	2900	2620	2380	2160	2802	2290	1890	1550	0.6	2.5	6.3
7mm Mauser (7x57) Super-X and Super-Speed	175	SP	2490	2170	1900	1680	2410	1830	1400	1100	0.8	3.7	9.5
*7mm Remington Magnum Super-X	150	PP(SP)	3260	2970	2700	2450	3540	2930	2430	1990	0.4	2.0	4.9
*7mm Remington Magnum Super-X	175	PP(SP)	3070	2720	2400	2120	3660	2870	2240	1750	0.5	2.4	6.1
†30 Carbine	110	HSP	1980	1540	1230	1040	955	575	370	260	1.4	7.5	21.7
30-30 Winchester Super-X and Super-Speed	150	OPE(HP)	2410	2020	1700	1430	1930	1360	960	680	0.9	4.2	11.0
30-30 Winchester Super-X and Super-Speed	150	PP(SP)	2410	2020	1700	1430	1930	1360	960	680	0.9	4.2	11.0
30-30 Winchester Super-X and Super-Speed	150	ST(Exp)	2410	2020	1700	1430	1930	1360	960	680	0.9	4.2	11.0
30-30 Winchester Super-X and Super-Speed	170	PP(SP)	2220	1890	1630	1410	1860	1350	1000	750	1.2	4.6	12.5
30-30 Winchester Super-X and Super-Speed	170	ST(Exp)	2220	1890	1630	1410	1860	1350	1000	750	1.2	4.6	12.5
30 Remington Super-X and Super-Speed	170	PP(SP)	2120	1820	1560	1350	1700	1250	920	690	1.1	5.3	14.0
30-06 Springfield Super-X and Super-Speed	110	PSP	3370	2830	2350	1920	2770	1960	1350	900	0.5	2.2	6.0
30-06 Springfield Super-X and Super-Speed	125	PSP	3200	2810	2450	2120	2840	2190	1660	1250	0.5	2.2	5.6
30-06 Springfield Super-X and Super-Speed	150	PP(SP)	2970	2620	2300	2010	2930	2290	1760	1340	0.6	2.5	6.5
30-06 Springfield Super-X and Super-Speed	150	ST(Exp)	2970	2670	2400	2130	2930	2370	1920	1510	0.6	2.4	6.1
30-06 Springfield Super-X and Super-Speed	180	PP(SP)	2700	2330	2010	1740	2910	2170	1610	1210	0.7	3.1	8.3
30-06 Springfield Super-X and Super-Speed	180	ST(Exp)	2700	2470	2250	2040	2910	2440	2020	1660	0.7	2.9	7.0
*30-06 Springfield Super-Match and Wimbledon Cup	180	FMCBT	2700	2520	2350	2190	2910	2540	2200	1900	0.6	2.8	6.7
*30-06 Springfield Super-X and Super-Speed	220	PP(SP)	2410	2120	1870	1670	2840	2190	1710	1360	0.8	3.9	9.8
*30-40 Krag Super-X	220	ST(Exp)	2180	1920	1680	1460	2320	1800	1380	1040	0.8	3.7	9.2
*30-40 Krag Super-X	180	PP(SP)	2470	2120	1830	1590	2440	1790	1340	1010	0.8	3.8	9.9

Cartridge	Wt. Grs.	Bullet Type	Velocity (fps)				Energy (ft. lbs.)				Mid-Range Trajectory (inches)		
			Muzzle	100 yds.	200 yds.	300 yds.	Muzzle	100 yds.	200 yds.	300 yds.	100 yds.	200 yds.	300 yds.
*30-40 Krag Super-X	180	ST(Exp)	2470	2250	2040	1850	2440	2020	1660	1370	0.8	3.5	8.5
*30-40 Krag Super-X	220	ST(Exp)	2200	1990	1800	1630	2360	1930	1580	1300	1.0	4.4	11.0
300 Winchester Magnum Super-X and Super-Speed	150	PP(SP)	3400	3050	2730	2430	3850	3100	2480	1970	0.4	1.9	4.8
300 Winchester Magnum Super-X and Super-Speed	180	PP(SP)	3070	2850	2640	2440	3770	3250	2790	2380	0.5	2.1	5.3
300 Winchester Magnum Super-X and Super-Speed	220	ST(Exp)	2720	2490	2270	2060	3620	3030	2520	2070	0.6	2.9	6.9
300 H&H Magnum Super-X and Super-Speed	150	ST(Exp)	3190	2870	2580	2300	3390	2740	2220	1760	0.5	2.1	5.2
300 H&H Magnum Super-X and Super-Speed	180	ST(Exp)	2920	2670	2440	2220	3400	2850	2380	1970	0.6	2.4	5.8
300 H&H Magnum Super-X and Super-Speed	220	ST(Exp)	2620	2370	2150	1940	3350	2740	2260	1840	0.7	3.1	7.7
300 Savage Super-X and Super-Speed	150	PP(SP)	2670	2350	2060	1800	2370	1840	1410	1080	0.7	3.2	8.0
300 Savage Super-X and Super-Speed	150	ST(Exp)	2670	2390	2130	1890	2370	1900	1510	1190	0.7	3.0	7.6
300 Savage Super-X and Super-Speed	180	PP(SP)	2370	2040	1760	1520	2240	1660	1240	920	0.9	4.1	10.5
300 Savage Super-X and Super-Speed	180	ST(Exp)	2370	2160	1960	1770	2240	1860	1530	1250	0.9	3.7	9.2
303 Savage Super-X and Super-Speed	190	PP(SP)	1980	1680	1440	1250	1650	1190	875	660	1.3	6.2	15.5
†303 British Super-Speed	180	PP(SP)	2540	2300	2090	1900	2580	2120	1750	1440	0.7	3.3	8.2
308 Winchester Super-X and Super-Speed	110	PSP	3340	2810	2340	1920	2730	1930	1340	900	0.5	2.2	6.0
308 Winchester Super-X and Super-Speed	125	PSP	3100	2740	2430	2160	2670	2080	1640	1300	0.5	2.3	5.9
308 Winchester Super-X and Super-Speed	150	PP(SP)	2860	2520	2210	1930	2730	2120	1630	1240	0.6	2.7	7.0
308 Winchester Super-X and Super-Speed	150	ST(Exp)	2860	2570	2300	2050	2730	2200	1760	1400	0.6	2.6	6.5
308 Winchester Super-X and Super-Speed	180	PP(SP)	2610	2250	1940	1680	2720	2020	1500	1130	0.7	3.4	8.9
308 Winchester Super-X and Super-Speed	180	ST(Exp)	2610	2390	2170	1970	2720	2280	1870	1540	0.7	3.1	7.4
308 Winchester Super-X and Super-Speed	200	ST(Exp)	2450	2210	1980	1770	2670	2170	1750	1400	0.8	3.6	9.0
32 Winchester Special Super-X and Super-Speed	170	PP(SP)	2280	1870	1560	1330	1960	1320	920	665	1.0	4.8	13.0
32 Winchester Special Super-X and Super-Speed	170	ST(Exp)	2280	1870	1560	1330	1960	1320	920	665	1.0	4.8	13.0
32 Remington Super-X and Super-Speed	170	ST(Exp)	2120	1760	1460	1220	1700	1170	805	560	1.1	5.3	14.5
32-20 Winchester (Oilproof)	100	L, Lead	1290	1060	940	840	370	250	195	155	3.3	15.5	38.0
32-20 Winchester (Oilproof)	100	SP	1290	1060	940	840	370	250	195	155	3.3	15.5	38.0
†8mm Mauser (8x57; 7.9) Super-Speed	170	PP(SP)	2570	2140	1790	1520	2490	1730	1210	870	0.8	3.9	10.5
338 Winchester Magnum Super-X and Super-Speed	200	PP(SP)	3000	2690	2410	2170	4000	3210	2580	2090	0.5	2.4	6.0
338 Winchester Magnum Super-X and Super-Speed	250	ST(Exp)	2700	2430	2180	1940	4050	3280	2640	2090	0.7	3.0	7.4
338 Winchester Magnum Super-X and Super-Speed	300	ST(Exp)	2450	2160	1910	1690	4000	3110	2430	1900	0.8	3.7	9.5
†348 Winchester Super-Speed	200	ST(Exp)	2530	2220	1940	1680	2840	2190	1670	1250	0.7	3.6	9.0
35 Remington Super-X and Super-Speed	200	PP(SP)	2100	1710	1390	1160	1950	1300	860	605	1.2	6.0	16.5
35 Remington Super-X and Super-Speed	200	ST(Exp)	2100	1710	1390	1160	1950	1300	860	605	1.2	6.0	16.5
351 Winchester Self-Loading (Oilproof)	180	SP	1850	1560	1310	1140	1370	975	685	520	1.5	7.8	21.5
358 Winchester (8.8mm) Super-X and Super-Speed	200	ST(Exp)	2530	2210	1910	1640	2840	2160	1610	1190	0.8	3.6	9.4
358 Winchester (8.8mm) Super-X and Super-Speed	250	ST(Exp)	2250	2010	1780	1570	2810	2230	1760	1370	1.0	4.4	11.0
375 H&H Magnum Super-X and Super-Speed	270	PP(SP)	2740	2460	2210	1990	4500	3620	2920	2370	0.7	2.9	7.1
375 H&H Magnum Super-X and Super-Speed	300	ST(Exp)	2550	2280	2040	1830	4330	3460	2770	2230	0.7	3.3	8.3
†375 H&H Magnum Super-Speed	300	FMC	2550	2180	1860	1590	4330	3160	2300	1680	0.8	3.6	9.3
38-40 Winchester (Oilproof)	180	SP	1330	1070	960	850	705	455	370	290	3.2	15.0	36.5
*44 Magnum Super-X	240	HSP	1750	1350	1090	950	1630	970	635	480	1.8	9.4	26.0
44-40 Winchester	200	SP	1310	1050	940	830	760	490	390	305	3.3	15.0	36.5
†45-70 Government	405	SP	1320	1160	1050	990	1570	1210	990	880	2.9	13.0	32.5
*458 Winchester Magnum Super-Speed	500	FMC	2130	1910	1700	1520	5040	4050	3210	2570	1.1	4.8	12.0
†458 Winchester Magnum Super-Speed	510	SP	2130	1840	1600	1400	5140	3830	2900	2220	1.1	5.1	13.5

*—Winchester Brand Only
†—Western Brand Only
HSP—Hollow Soft Point
PEP—Positive Expanding Point

PSP—Pointed Soft Point
PP(SP)—Power-Point Soft Point
FMC—Full Metal Case

SP—Soft Point
HP—Hollow Point
L—Lubaloy

OPE—Open Point Expanding
ST(Exp)—Silvertip Expanding
FMCBT—Full Metal Case Boat Tail

(From 1972 Winchester-Western catalog.)

CHAPTER 6

Small Game Rifles

The .22 rimfires

No matter if a hunter is primarily concerned with elk hunting in the Alpine meadows of the Rocky Mountains, still-hunting whitetail deer in Maine, long range varmint sniping or just tree squirrel in a farm woodlot, his most important field rifle is a .22 rimfire. It is not only a beautiful caliber in its own right for small game hunting, it also has a definite place as an understudy and stand-in for all the different calibers carried afield.

The high degree of skill required for clean, humane kills in all phases of hunting is usually the product of .22 rifle shooting.

There is no line of demarcation where a hunter can say this is big game shooting skill. This is squirrel shooting skill. All field shooting skills are related, just as all stalking, sign reading, and woodcraft are related—just as all food and cover preferences have about the same requirements.

Why more hunters do not consider their field shooting rifles as a related battery is one of the mysteries. Why arms manufacturers feel they have fulfilled their obligation to the cause of hunting when they make a big or small game rifle without duplicating it exactly with another rifle, so hunters have similar rifles for all their shooting, is equally mysterious. Someday, somewhere, a custom gunsmith will begin building rifles in series—a .30/06 bolt action, perhaps, a beautiful .222 Remington, and a .22 rimfire, not as individual rifles, but as a field battery. They will be stocked alike, have the same length bolt throw, sights, weight, trigger pull. He will also make a battery of suitable calibers for both the lever actions and slide actions. When this occurs, hunters will beat a path to his door, as wide and as well worn as the path leading to the house of the man making the better mouse trap.

It would be nice to know that you could plunk your iron men down for a small rifle and when you decided to take a big game hunting trip you could get a rifle of suitable caliber that would take advantage of all the skill and confidence developed small game hunting. And it would be an excellent conservation measure, too.

I have a Marlin 39A lever action tucked under my arm when I hunt the river bottoms, where the briar grown brush patches catch the first sheen of autumn frost and there are cottontails on my mind. This hunting is not a backhanded effort, without relationship to all field shooting. Cottontail rabbit shooting puts the same premium on fast rifle handling and accuracy as big game hunting. The rifle has much in common with big game rifles designed for the touch and go of shooting deer in heavy cover.

A morning's rabbit hunt will turn up targets at twenty-five to seventy-five yards, very typical ranges for all hunting from small game to deer or elk.

Most of the shooting is off-hand. Again, that is typical. When I get a near miss as the game is feeding along the marge of those briar patches, a second shot is at a fleeting target where all the speed and accuracy of a snapshot is never more than enough for a clean kill. (Remember that buck you surprised on a hardwood ridge last autumn? That line could have been written about your shooting.) Small game shooting, such as I have along those autumn river bottoms is exciting shooting in its own right, and from the standpoint of big game shooting skill, very rewarding.

In an over-all consideration of small game hunting with .22 rifles, big game shooting must be taken into consideration. Small game rifles are not subordinated to big game rifles, nor is small game hunting less important. But in order to spread shooting skills wide enough to include big game hunting, small game rifles must be selected with this over-all consideration in mind.

Select a big game rifle *action,* complement it all the way down the line, and you will come to your small game hunting with an excellent choice of rifles, for all hunting is basically the same.

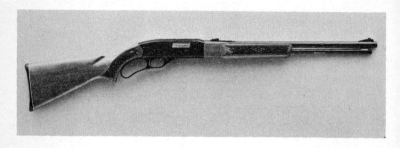

A hammerless lever-action combination, the Win. Model 88 (above) for big game and the Win. Model 250 .22 for small game, pests and plinking.

A good pair of bolt-actions—The Remington Model 700 (above) for big game and the Remington Model 581 for .22 use.

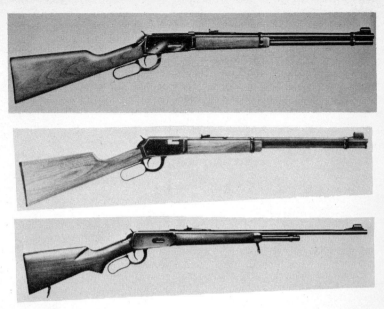

Exposed hammer lever-action rifles in the Winchester line that offer good matching combinations. Either the Model 94 (above) or the Model 64 (below) in center-fire calibers and features having a counterpart in the .22 Model 9422 (center).

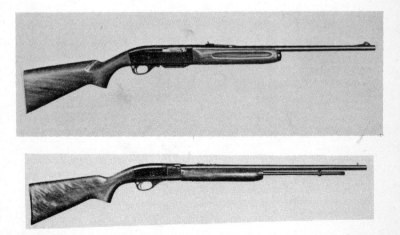

For those favoring semiautomatics, here's a good combination; Remington's Model 740A big game rifle (above) and the Remington Model 552 .22.

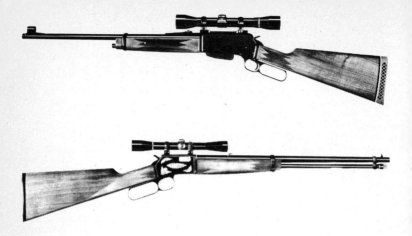

Exposed hammer lever-action rifles can be had in the Browning line, too, the high-power rifle (above) and the BL-.22 rifle (below).

Another possible bolt-action combination, Mossberg's Model 810 big game rifle (above) and the Model 341 .22 (below).

In making the selection, plenty of horse trading will have to be done or else it is no true hunting rifle, but a specialized firearm for just one type of shooting. Sometimes a bit of target range accuracy should be swapped for other qualities—ranging ability traded for ease of handling, and speed in getting off a second shot. After the trading is done, a hunter usually finds that, from the standpoint of practical field shooting, those trades which widened groups on targets have narrowed them in the touch and go of field shooting.

When a big whitetail buck crashes out of his snug bed in the top of a windfall, *some certain rifle caliber and action* in your hands will have just the proper amount of compromise in its makeup to be highly woods accurate, and you will roll your trophy with plenty to spare.

The essentials of this rifle are no different than those of a .22 rimfire which you have found right for rolling a cottontail or a squirrel. Field shooting accuracy has a lot to do with a short range shot when you are stepping under a snow laden hemlock and a buck crashes out. It has a lot to do with one shot kills when you are sitting with your back to an autumn touched oak, watching for grey squirrel.

Other factors being equal, which they seldom are, a brush hunter has advantages in a lever or pump action rifle as a basis for his field shooting battery. Under the compelling necessity of field shooting, when a buck crashes out of that windfall cedar, stained antlers gleaming in the pale sunlight, accuracy has an element of expediency more important than target group size.

In mountain shooting, long range mule deer shooting, elk or rock chuck shooting, accuracy is measured in sensible inches, not expediency. A hunter could well trade some of the advantages of a lever or pump action for the added accuracy and ranging qualities of a bolt action rifle. All rifle actions have some advantages, but you cannot have them all in just one type action, nor can you expect to come to your hunting with the highest degree of field shooting skill of which you are capable if you constantly switch from one action to another.

See what a whale of a compromise there is in selecting field rifles? See how utterly impossible it is to say that a .224 Weatherby driving a 48 grain bullet at 3750 feet a second, is a better woodchuck rifle than a 6.5mm using a 140 grain soft point at 2450 feet a second?

I hunt elk, deer, squirrel, occasionally woodchuck. During the winter, when other seasons are closed or my quarry is snugged down for the cold spell, I love the high brushy ridges where snowshoe rabbits range. This hunting, from the smallest to the largest game is equally satisfying. It requires equal rifle skills, and matched rifles.

A bull elk bugling in a canyon some cold foggy November morning has its moments. So does a session in the hardwoods with a .22 rifle, hunting squirrel. Flushing blue grouse from the huckleberry brush and snipping their heads off when they perch in the second growth is thrilling hunting.

Here is my basic rifle outfit from squirrel to elk. First, and most important, is the before mentioned Marlin 39A lever action with its Micro-groove rifling. I use this rifle constantly the year around. It is the sweetest shooting, easiest handled .22 rifle I have ever used. There is a beautiful compromise of barrel length, weight and stocking for field shooting. It has a nice hand-filling forearm, a stock with very comfortable dimensions for snapshooting, kneeling or sitting positions.

Here are the essentials of that stocking: overall length of stock from trigger to center of buttplate 13¼ inches. Buttplate 5 inches long. Pitch (angle at which buttplate is set on stock) 3 inches. From line of sight to comb of stock 1⅝ inches. From line of sight to heel of buttplate 2½ inches.

Next is a now obsolete Model 71 lever action, .348 caliber. This is the big game kingpin of my battery. All skill acquired off-season is directed toward using it during autumn big game seasons. I have fired only nine shots at deer with it during the last eight big game seasons. Eight bucks were bagged. Obviously, this amount of shooting contributes very little except confidence to the skill required to make those kills. There must be a pickup in the small game fields to compensate for the lack of shooting one gets in big game hunting. Big game seasons are too short, bag limits too restricted to actually acquire field shooting proficiency there.

What action? That question has plagued every hunter going afield, regardless of the game he has in mind. Is there some one action with which you would be better armed for all hunting? The answer is an unqualified "yes." Just as sure as sure, there is one type rifle with which you will do your best shooting, just as there is very apt to be one certain big game caliber which will deliver best for you.

Proper action must not only be measured against field shooting situations, but against the temperament of the hunter himself.

Some hunters require the steadying influence of a good smooth working bolt action for their best shooting. The very mechanics of manually operating a rifle tends to more accurate shooting, though accuracy is usually associated with sights. Remember, speed of fire has no inherent virtue, unless there is complementing accuracy. Sometimes hunters need an action which will slow them down to acquire this accuracy. Sometimes certain temperaments require actions which will speed up their rate of fire. It all depends.

The sleight of hand, subconscious operation of a slide action may be the one thing which will contribute the necessary accuracy to your field shooting. It depends on the hunter. It is faster than a bolt action. But that isn't its chief virtue, smoothness is, and the fact that sights are not off the target during reloading. With some hunters it has just the proper division of work and concentration for accurate field shooting.

Somewhat the same thing can be said for the lever action. Again, it is faster than a bolt. But, again, that is not its chief virtue. The smoothness of operation and the steadying influence of its easily-learned manipulation are its chief merits.

Both the slide action and the lever action can be more easily mastered than a bolt action. But once a bolt action *is* mastered, it has plenty of merit for any type of field shooting from snapshooting to long range varmint sniping.

The automatic is definitely the most tricky action of the lot to handle properly in game shooting. A hunter of nervous temperament, under the stress of taking running shots, has no business with an automatic rifle in his hands. The tendency to spray the landscape with a magazine full of ammunition is almost irresistible. His best bet would be a smooth working bolt action or a lever action for their steadying influence. It is even questionable whether he is temperamentally fitted to use a slide action rifle.

By the same token a hunter of phlegmatic temperament is often greatly handicapped with a bolt action, lever or slide action. His best choice would naturally be an automatic rifle, both for small game and big game shooting. He would be

The Win. Model 100 big game rifle in semiautomatic action can be paired in the same maker's line with a .22 such as the Model 190 or 290.

much more accurate, and speedy enough to master just about any gunning situation his hunting turns up.

There are other factors in selecting the proper action, as you shall presently see—field conditions in which some actions fit like a hunting glove. But hunter-rifle relationship comes first.

Lever actions are wonderful woods rifles. For a still hunter with his mind on deer and elk in heavy cover, there is no better action. It is surprising how well this action fits into most small game hunting too. .300 Savage, .35 Rem. Marlin, .250/3000 Savage, .348 Winchester. These calibers at one end of the hunting trail, and matched with a .22 Marlin 39A at the other end, and you are not far wrong for any type of shooting from squirrel to elk.

There are other conditions and other actions. A hunter who has used a bolt action extensively on the target range gains nothing by trying to go to a pump action or lever because they are better for woods shooting of deer. He will be much better served by procuring a bolt action understudy and using it in the small game field to iron out his shooting, de-

Marlin Model 56 Levermatic .22; this could be paired with several high-power lever-action rifles for big game use and even go well for those who like the Savage M99 for big game hunting.

veloping subconscious habits which take over under the stress and excitement of game shooting.

Bolt action .22 calibers give the small game hunter a very wide selection from which to choose. Best, of couse, is a custom stocked rifle based on either the Remington Model 541-S, or Winchester Model 52 action, with the stocking and weight exactly that of your bolt action long range sniping rifle, and your big game bolt action.

Hunters who cannot acquire custom stocked jobs still have several alternatives. The Marlin Model 81C bolt action, Remington Model 581, Winchester Model 320, Mossberg Model 340B. All these are in addition to the Winchester Model 52 Sporter, the best designed field gun of the lot—if you are lucky enough to find one.

One other bolt action must be mentioned, however, a specialized rifle which my hunting gang swears by. This is the "coon gun," Mossberg bolt action Carbine, Model 142: 18 inch barrel, weight 5 pounds trailside. "Coon gun" is not its official title, but a name bestowed by this gang of night roving raccoon hunters who are out almost every night when a full autumn moon silvers the cover and frost rims on the fields. When they start out, it is an all night affair. So a rifle must have exceptional portability, as well as good practical accuracy to receive their endorsement. Mossberg's light bolt action carbine fits these requirements like a glove. The latest version of this rifle is the Model 342K.

A hunter using a Remington Model 760 slide action for deer, a pump action shotgun for upland bird shooting and in the duck blinds should never consider anything for squirrel shooting except a slide action .22. A Remington Model 121 or 572 is about tops. It has enough weight for steady holding, a semi-beavertail forearm. It is nicely stocked, and usually comes from the factory with a crisp trigger pull. Winchester Models 61 and 270 are also a good choice for tree squirrels, rabbit hunting and targets of opportunity during the summer months. The Model 61 has good stocking, but is a half pound lighter than the Remington Model 121. And light weight is the curse of most .22 rifles, unless they are for some specialized purpose, such as the "coon gun."

Both the Remington Model 121 and the Winchester Model 61 are superior woods rifles in the .22 Special caliber. The .22 RF Magnum has more killing power than a standard .22. It

Perhaps the only "old-fashioned" .22 exposed hammer pump repeater available today via import is this Garcia-Rossi "Gallery Model" (made abroad).

drives a 40 grain bullet at a muzzle velocity of 1550 feet a second, with a muzzle energy of 355 pounds. The .22 long rifle, in comparison, has a velocity of 1335 feet a second with a 40 grain bullet, giving a muzzle energy of 158 pounds.

It is unfortunate that the .22 Special caliber, in both the Remington and Winchester, is now obsolete. But quite often very good rifles in this caliber can be picked up secondhand.

The .22 RF Magnum is splendid on tree squirrel. That extra bit of energy puts you on your target with more clean killing hits, especially when body shots must be taken. It is also more deadly on running jacks, cottontails and ground squirrel. It is maybe a hair not quite as accurate as the regular .22, all factors considered, but it would take a very skilled shot to find any difference in accuracy, even on a target range. In the field, limitations of range will cancel out clean killing before any inherent inaccuracy become apparent. What better can be said of any rifle?

Winchester Model 62 (discontinued) and Model 9422 are the only American-made small game rifles, other than the Marlin Model 39A, with an outside hammer. This feature makes it a favorite with many experienced woodsmen because it is such a simple, easy to operate safety. With the hammer set at half cock, it is perfectly safe to carry with a load in the chamber. At the same time it is exceptionally fast to get into action when a rabbit hound flushes a bunny from the security of a briar patch, or a squirrel rattles through the fallen autumn leaves, heading for a den tree.

A hunter devoted to an automatic shotgun or big game rifle has several .22 automatics from which to select his small game hunting rifle. Although now superseded by the M49, the Marlin Models 88C or 89C are excellent choices. Both have

Shown is the Ithaca X-5 Lightning .22 semiautomatic rifle with tubular magazine; the same rifle is available in a clip version.

Marlin's accurate Micro-Groove rifling. The Model 88C has a
tubular magazine, loading through the butt-plate, the 89C is a
clip loader. Using this rifle one autumn while hunting tree
squirrel, I found it very accurate and practical for running
shots when a big grey squirrel was crossing through the tops
of the oaks, a very exciting target. On another occasion, when
Grant Hartwell and I were giving our autumn deer shooting a
final polishing on ground squirrel before the big game season
opened, I used Marlin's Model 88C for the day. Our hunting
rule this time was to take nothing but running shots, for
within weeks we would be in the autumn deer woods, catfooting along the brushy ridges where bucks had horned the
low growing red cedar, mountain willow and ash.

We flushed our squirrels and tried for a kill as they scur-
ried for their dens. That meant short range snapshooting, with
plenty of careful stalking to get within reasonable range before our quarry got under way. What a beautiful, exciting day
of shooting we had! What wonderful preseason shooting in
preparation for deer hunting in heavy cover!

That Marlin automatic certainly complemented the day in
every respect, giving me good accuracy—and not a malfunc-
tion all day, even though I used both regular and high-speed
ammunition.

Both the Marlin Model 88C and 89C have sufficient weight
for good steady holding, weighing in at 6¾ pounds. The
stocking is full and mansized, very closely duplicating the
excellent stocking on the Marlin Model 39A lever action.

Mossberg, Model 151K .22 caliber automatic and their
newer M351C are also excellent choices for a small game
rifle. These are well stocked and heavy enough for close,
steady holding, weighing about 7 pounds. Savage's version of

the .22 automatic is another good plinking rifle. In addition, there are several others available which will give entire satisfaction at reasonable ranges. But Marlin and Mossberg, it seems to me, are more mansized in their stocking, come closer to approximating the dimension of hunting rifles.

Another fine combination by Remington, the Model 760 big game rifle (above) and the Model 572 .22 pump (below).

PART III

Sights
and Sighting In

CHAPTER 7

Sights With A Purpose
The iron sights

A soft whisper of dawn wind accented the autumn stillness, and stripped an occasional leaf from the maples to drop it gently on the small stream at the foot of the hardwood ridge. It was such a day as hunters dream about. Woods were gold, brown and incarnadine with the first touch of autumn, and grey squirrels were at their nut harvesting in the wide spreading oaks.

When I topped out on a ridge, the sun was still scarcely two hands' breadth above the forest. A whole golden day lay before me to be spent still hunting squirrel. What more could one ask than this?

I moved slowly along a hogsback, my .25/35 tucked under my arm. I listened for acorns ticking down through the trees. I combed the tops of those oaks with my binoculars, watching for the tip-off of a feeding squirrel. First shot was at a grey in the crotch of a high fork, with just the tip of his head showing occasionally as he worked at his nut cutting. I dropped into a sitting position, leaned back until I felt the firm pressure of a tree bole against my shoulder. At the shot there was no action for a moment, then my quarry kicked himself free of his perch and came tumbling down from limb to limb to lie beside a moss covered granite outcropping.

Next shot came almost immediately at another grey scurrying across the forest carpet, making for a white, bleached oak, pockmarked with woodpecker holes. I rolled him with a body shot. Then, picking up my squirrels I move along the ridge. It was shooting very typical of all tree squirrel hunting. Ranges were from a long fifty yards to a short fifty feet.

My mid-range handloads had been carefully sighted in at fifty yards, using a 111 grain gas check bullet, 18 grains of Hi-Vel, for a velocity of 1880 feet a second, a very killing combination on squirrel without too much destruction.

Nothing which might add to the success of this autumn day afield had been slighted. Each hunting element from rifle selection down to the last granule of powder had to make some worthwhile contribution.

Not the least of those contributions were the iron sights with which my rifle was equipped. For a hunter never has an advantage to spare in squirrel shooting, any more than he has when a canny old buck comes boiling out of a laurel thicket.

Sights: Williams Foolproof Receiver sight, using a disk of ⅜ inch over all diameter, with a .125 inner hole. The front sight was a Redfield Sourdough. This combination is an almost unbeatable iron sight combination for anything from squirrel or cottontail to deer. They merit careful consideration when outfitting a small game field rifle for autumn squirrel, with the idea of transferring shooting skills to the big game coverts later in the season.

Williams' Foolproof receiver sight has the exceptional merit of being, as its name exemplifies, totally foolproof for that type of individual who must be constantly examining rifles about camp, twisting adjustment knobs on rifle sight, just to assure himself you *do* carry sights capable of adjustment. Sighted in, Williams' Foolproof receiver sights can be locked, and neither windage nor elevation can be changed without a small screwdriver, an excellent feature in a rear hunting sight.

It has micrometer adjustment for both windage and elevation, so several different bullet weights and loadings can be calibrated and noted for future sight setting data, without the compelling necessity of additional sighting-in each time a loading is changed to meet certain hunting requirements. For example, I have midrange readings for my squirrel loads, my long range full power sniping loads. In shifting from one load requirement to another it is a simple matter to re-set my sights.

The Williams' Foolproof receiver sight has one other advantage, which, I suppose, must be classified as one of the intangibles of rifle shooting afield. Its streamlined appearance, with its lack of protruding elevation and windage knobs, makes it, as the old woodsman Al Lyman remarked, "look like you could hit something with it." In addition to that, there is another little nuance of accuracy in this streamlining. There is an added dividend in the lack of cluttering up of the bridge to obscure targets when the rifle is snapped to the shoulder on fast moving game.

Redfield's Sourdough front sight, the other part of this hunting sight combination, will give more uniform accuracy under varying light conditions than any front sight which I have tested over a period of twenty-five years of hunting. It is rugged beyond belief, a square gold bead set at an angle of 45 degree on a heavy steel stem.

The angle at which the bead is set, affords very uniform lighting under all field conditions. Most any front sight will give good hunter groups under ideal lighting. Very few will not change their center of impact as the lighting is changed. Their accuracy is not uniform from the poor lighting of early

The Williams Foolproof Receiver Sight. Note the uncluttered bridge of this very practical hunting sight. All windage and elevation adjustments are capable of being locked. This sight has the Williams aperture with gold-colored insert.

morning to the bright lighting of midday. The filtered light be-neath a heavy oak grove will give one center of impact, that of open woods another. But with Redfield's Sourdough, you have excellent accuracy all the way. Its square .070 wide gold bead is a large part of the answer. The rest of the answer is the uniform skylight caught by that 45 degree angle of the bead.

The square gold bead cuts directly across your target with a razor sharp edge—no blurring. So there is much less tend-ency to scatter shots up and down because different lighting gives different appearances to the front sight, something which constantly occurs with a conventional round gold bead.

A round gold bead will not only scatter shots up and down your target, but there is also a decided tendency to shoot away from the light. This is caused by a hunter subcon-sciously aligning the brightest part of his bead in the center of his aperture. When the sun is on the left, lighting up the left side of the bead, the bullet will go to the right of the aiming point. This error of aim is enough to completely miss a squir-rel's head at thirty-five or forty yards. At longer ranges of a hundred yards or over, it may be as much as six to eight inches.

If your rifle comes equipped with a rounded gold bead, a great deal of improvement in accuracy can be made with a small flat file. By filing, the face of the bead can be flattened to give more uniform lighting. The top can be flattened also to give more uniform grouping with much less tendency to scatter shots up and down the target.

A $\frac{1}{16}$ inch bead can be shaped in this manner. Those smaller than this give you too little on which to work. Larger, so-called semi-jack beads are usually made of ivory, and are not easily worked into acceptable field shooting shapes. Best solution, of course, is to buy a square gold bead and replace the outmoded round beads.

The Redfield receiver sights, series 70, with hunter adjust-ing knobs are very good selections for small game hunting rifles. They have coin slotted knobs for easy sight adjustment, and once set, cannot be turned by hand, a very good hunting feature on any adjustable sight other than those used strictly for target range shooting. The Redfield receiver sights Series 102 are very practical hunting sights where no more than one type load will be used in a rifle. These have no micrometer

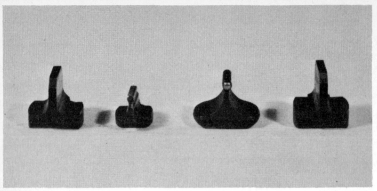

Some typical rifle front sights showing both square and rounded beads.

adjustments, and where more than one type load is used, they would prove a handicap. A hunter would be much better off to pay the difference between these and their series 70 which have nice click adjustments of a quarter minute of angle, windage and elevation.

Micrometer adjustment, while very handy, is not essential on a .22 rimfire small game hunting rifle. Williams make a very inexpensive receiver sight for most .22 plinking rifles. Many models of this sight are of the extension type, putting the sight close to the shooter's eye, giving him a very good sighting picture, and superb accuracy on squirrel and kindred game.

But to get back to our squirrel hunting under those oaks. My rear sight had one very essential part to which most small game hunters give all too little consideration—aperture size for field shooting. To be right, it must meet at least five requirements for shooting anything from ground squirrel to big game.

My first two shots, typical of all squirrel shooting that day, exemplify the problem. The one at a squirrel with just part of its head showing required precision. The shot taken at a running squirrel not only required precision, but also had an element of speedy snapshooting. Not all size apertures have enough shooting latitude to have performed well on both these shots. A hunting aperture must be able to quickly pick up a fleeting target, be it squirrel, rabbit or deer. It must also

have the ability to resolve targets under poor forest lighting—
early morning and late evening shooting.

The problem actually starts with our eyes. The pupil of the
eye is the window through which light passes into the eye. It
varies in size according to the brightness of the light falling
upon it. Under intense light it may become as small as .07 of
an inch. When light is less bright it will be nearer ⅛ inch in
diameter. Hunters using a sight aperture much smaller than
this needlessly handicap themselves.

Putting the yardstick of field shooting on the problem of
proper aperture size, a hunter arrives at about the same answer. A large ⅛ inch hole, while excellent for the squirrel
woods from the standpoint of light, it is no less efficient for a
fast catching of aim in snapshooting at running targets, such
as that grey making for the security of a den tree. It will serve,
too, snap-shooting rabbit, ground squirrel or deer. In addition,
it will turn in a good score on the more precise shots, where
light is not the main consideration.

A Tradewinds snapshooter aperture receiver sight on a 6.5 x 55mm Hus-
qvarna big game rifle as set up for deer hunting in thick brush. You can
"bark" a squirrel while it is holding to the bole of a tree by shooting
directly under its head. For safety reasons such shooting shouldn't be at-
tempted, however, in the vicinity of settled communities. This is probably
the most sturdy receiver sight of the lot and is adjustable for both windage
and elevation. By mounting the scope slightly higher than usual, the sight
can be left on the rifle while the scope is used.

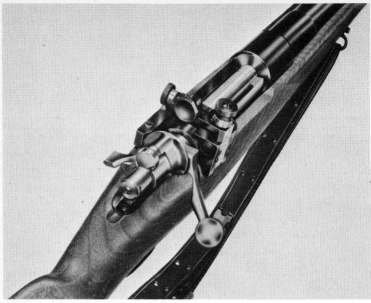

While this is a very good target sight, the aperture is too small for hunting and the sight's bridge is cluttered with windage and elevation adjustment knobs. Target disc aperture can be removed, however, leaving a large open peep and a number of hunters use it that way for big game and varmint shooting.

The outside diameter of ⅜ inch gives you a sight which is in balance with just the proper amount of rim around the aperture to insure a quick confident catching of aim under all circumstances. There is not enough rim, however, to slow you down, obscure the target, or blank out any of the essential territory around the game.

Smaller aperture sizes than ⅛, such as the .050, with an outer diameter of ⅝ inch, the type most inexperienced hunters select for field shooting, are definitely target range equipment, and have no place afield.

Best bet is to select an aperture for the *poorest light* and the *fastest shooting*. You will not be wrong for any shooting where a peep sight can be used, from squirrel to deer to elk.

A consideration of iron sights is never complete without some notice of open sights. And, let it be whispered, all the experts to the contrary, for certain types of shooting open sights are very fast, and with plenty of practical accuracy. They are not the best selection, though, for all eyes, or all hunting. It really takes very keen young eyes for good field shooting with open sights.

As eyes grow older, and the tendency to farsightedness becomes more pronounced, a hunter using open sights finds his rear sight very fuzzy and indistinct.

Best arrangement of open sights I have ever shot was a Redfield Sourdough, square gold bead front sight, a straight bar rear sight, with a white diamond centered on it for aiming. Another very good arrangement is the same Redfield Sourdough, and a complementing square notched rear—the Patridge type sight.

Of the several woodsmen who go in for open sights, I have yet to find one who uses them in the traditional manner of "drawing a bead" in the rear notch, with its unholy tendency to overshoot or undershoot, depending on the light. Most hunters use a full bead above the ear notch or crossbar, with the exception of the Patridge type sights. These are used with the square bead just filling the rear notch. Open

This Williams open rear sight can be adjusted for both elevation and windage.

sights used as they should be, are fairly accurate for short range squirrel shooting and big game shooting in heavy cover. In addition, they are very fast. But for long range game shooting, a hunter is greatly handicapped with open sights on his rifle.

How fast are they?

When open sights are matched against the speed of a sleight-of-hand snapshooting hunter using a large inner hole aperture peep of the type outlined, the speed of open sights is no great advantage. They are very little faster than peep sights in the hands of equally skilled rifle shots.

Measured from the standpoint of practical field shooting at all ranges and under all light conditions, open sights are no bargain. Just about anything which can be done with open sights can be accomplished better with a good receiver peep sight. In addition, proper aperture sights tend to condition a hunter for telescope sights. And that is important in the overall consideration of field shooting, for it tends to make a hunter an all-round, practical field shot.

CHAPTER 8

Sights With A Purpose

Telescope sights and mounts

When Art Richardson and I angled around those mountains on the prowl for ground squirrel, jack rabbits and other targets of opportunity, our rifles were scope sighted. When I worked the autumn ridges for grey squirrel, my .25/35 sported iron sights. These two type sights, receiver and scope, complement each other in small and large game shooting. A woodsman must become top hole proficient with both or his ability to keep his hunt in hand is drastically limited. There are times during stormy weather when receiver sights are much more efficient than scope sights. There are times, when making long range shots, that nothing will bring out the accuracy potential of a rifle like a good scope sight.

There are many hunting situations in which either scope or receiver sights will serve with equal facility. I not only use my .25/35 and receiver sights on tree squirrel; there are times when I prowl the hardwood ridges with another beautiful squirrel outfit, a Model 39A Marlin .22 lever action, scoped with a Bushnell Scope Chief 2½X. There are other times when I hunt ground squirrel with a precision 8X scope riding the receiver of a .222 Remington Sako. On occasion as the big game season approaches, for a final polishing of field shooting, I mount a 3X scope on my old Model 71, .348 Winchester.

These calibers and these scopes are not the best possible selections when measured against some certain segment of a day's shooting. Each is a compromise covering a wide spread of field use most efficiently, from short range to long. All of them are excellent selections when measured against the

over-all requirements of a day's hunting, more so when measured against the over-all requirements of a season's hunting
from big game to small.

Some riflemen contend that a scope of 8 power or greater
has no place except on a precision long range sniping outfit.
They feel that the high potential of the scope is wasted on a
rifle of lesser accuracy. Bosh!

I like to loaf through the hills at times, with a beautiful
Bushnell 8X scope on my .22 Model 39-A lever action Marlin.
This rifle, of course, is capable of a minute and three quarters
accuracy at one hundred yards, but it is not a long range rifle.
Scoped with an 8 power Bushnell it had a lot of qualifications not usually associated with .22 rimfire rifles. This 8
power scope is a beautiful glass, with a resolution capable of
separating a grey squirrel's whiskers at fifty yards. With you
can bring out the full accuracy potential of my Marlin Lever
action. *A good scope ups the accuracy potential of any
hunter.*

If you are doing a bit of precision shooting with a rifle capable of two minutes angle of accuracy at one hundred yards,
an 8 or 10 power scope is essential because you haven't any
accuracy to spare. A loss of an additional half minute of accuracy here may be more manifest in field results than in a rifle
capable of less than a minute of angle accuracy.

Just recently I used my 8X Bushnell Scope Chief on my
Model 64 Winchester lever action for shooting ground squirrel. This scope, and carefully handloaded ammunition made
my rifle equally accurate with the .257 Roberts, ranging out
beautifully for several long range kills. Longest shot was a
measured 205 yards for the .25/35, and 220 yards for the .257
Roberts. This later rifle using a K4 Weaver scope.

Hunters of any extended experience have preferences in
scopes. What does the average rifleman select when he buys a
scope for his small or large game hunting? One manufacturer's sales of quality scopes are as follows: 70 percent selected
4 power, 15 percent selected 2½ power, another 15 percent
selected 6 power. In the out and out sniping scopes, 8 and 10
power, 80 percent selected 10 power.

Power in scopes is probably the least understood of the
many factors a hunter must consider in selecting a scope.
Many hunters go to extremes. They mount 15 or even 20
power scopes on their varmint rifle under the mistaken idea

(Courtesy Bushnell)
Bushnell's 3X-8X variable power Scopechief .22 Riflescope model.

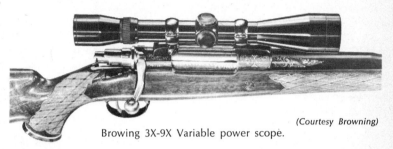

(Courtesy Browning)
Browing 3X-9X Variable power scope.

that power alone gives them a clear and more accurate sight picture. As you up the power in a scope sight, it becomes a more specialized instrument. It is doubtful if a scope of more than 10 power is of any advantage for any kind of field shooting.

Studies were made in the Bureau of Standards, by Dr. Francis E. Washer to determine the effect of magnification on accuracy of telescope pointing. His formula for calculating indoor error is as follows:

$$PES = \frac{4.962}{M} + .068$$

That will give you a probable error of aim between a 6X and a 20X scope of .508 seconds.

Studies also show that, while outdoor pointing has a greater error due to air turbulence, they add up to very little in relation to power. But they do show that power alone is a very small segment of the answer to accuracy. Power, to be right for field shooting, where a hunter wants to use the small game fields to develop shooting skills which are of some use hunting larger game, is a decided compromise.

Relative brightness, field of view, magnification, each element affects the whole. Primarily, a bright flat field with sharp definition and resolution is the hallmark of all good hunting scopes. Increased power using the same size objective lens means decreased relative brightness, in the field of view, other factors being equal.

Let's set up a standard of measurement for average field use, then find how many different scopes fit into the pattern. Obviously, a hunter wants a large bright field designed for the touch and go of snapshooting running jacks, cottontails, squirrel and woodchuck shooting. That adds up to many of the requirements of a big game hunting scope, but so much the better.

Relative brightness in a hunting scope shouldn't be below 45. This one requirement simplifies selection of small game hunting scopes by getting rid of a lot of borderline scopes the main virtue of which is their cheapness. A relative brightness of 60 not only gives plenty of light for late evening shooting, but a much larger field as well. As you increase power, without a corresponding increase in the clear opening of the objective lens, relative brightness is reduced.

The only exception to a large relative brightness requirement in hunting scopes is the out and out precision sniping scope of 8 or 10 power. Here, a bit of horse trading can be done because you will more than likely be using such scopes during midday at stationary targets.

Resolution and definition must be tops in hunting scopes. At best there is a limited amount of light used by the eye. During midday, under bright light, the eye pupil adjusts to about 2 or 3 millimeters. At dusk it enlarges to about 5 millimeters, or a relative brightness of 25. This indicates a scope exit pupil of at least 5.25 millimeters. But actually, one of 8 millimeters is much better because it is less critical as to eye placement in sighting. While eye accommodation is served by a relative brightness of 25, other factors of sighting are important for good all-around field performance.

As you up the power of a hunting scope, you not only cut down the relative brightness, if there is no corresponding increase in the size of objective lens, but the field of view as well. For the razzle-dazzle of fast moving small game shooting, it is very important to have a wide clear field of view, the larger the better.

Under uncertain light of early morning and late afternoon

in dense woods, a 32 foot field of view is none too much, 40 feet is still better. Those requirements of squirrel shooting, as well as rabbit and big game under poor light conditions, up the relative brightness of hunting scopes to 64 or better, depending on the power of the scope, other factors being equal. On occasion, when I take to the squirrel woods with a scope having less field of view than this, my shooting is, of a necessity, confined to stationary targets, an interesting way of squirrel shooting in its own right, but limited.

Sniping woodchuck or ground squirrel at long range, the field of view is less important. Another horse trade can be made here. The 3X scope, with its 40 feet field of view, while one of the best for all around shooting, is not as desirable for sniping as a more powerful scope. A 6X, 8X or a 10X, having a 30, 17 and 12 foot field of view is a much better choice.

Eye relief in hunting scopes cannot be divorced from either relative brightness, or field of view. Again, as you up the power of your scope by changing the objective, eye relief becomes shorter, more critical. Take the excellent line of Bushnell hunting scopes as an example. Eye relief in the 2½ power is 3 to 5 inches; field of view is 43 feet. Three power, eye relief 3 to 4¾ inches; field of view 40 feet. Four power, eye relief 3 to 4½ inches, field of view 33 feet. Six power, eye relief 3 to 4 inches, field of view 17 feet. Ten power, eye relief 2⅝ to 3½ inches, field of view 13 feet at a hundred yards.

For snapshooting at moving targets, there must be an eye relief spread of at least 3 to 4½ inches. When you snap your rifle to your shoulder, your eye is not always in the same precise place, even with the best custom stocking. Less eye relief than this slows you down.

Then, too, there is the problem of recoil. In rifles having heavy recoil, if one is shooting uphill, a scope with very little eye relief is brought dangerously close to the shooter's eye. Of course, in long range sniping, which is mostly a prone shooting show, this is not nearly as much of a problem. One has time to get into position, adjust a sling strap, hold steady and carefully, and recoil will not thrust the scope back as it would in fast snapshooting at moving game.

The most common reticle selected for hunting, according to the sales of one manufacturer, is the crosshairs. About 90 percent select them for their hunting rifles. These are excellent for all types of field shooting under a wide spread of lighting. However, with very fine crosshairs, such as most long range sniping scopes of 8 power or more have, it is very hard to properly center them on game in very late evening or early morning. Fine crosshairs blend with the gloomy background to an extent which makes them impracticable for late evening shooting. A medium crosshair, like a medium powered scope, is much the better choice for such uncertain light.

A dot and crosshair is also very good for all small and large game shooting. Here one has the problem of matching the dot to the power of the scope. A 4X, due to its greater magnification, requires a smaller dot than a 2½ power scope. A dot subtending 3 minutes of angle is excellent for snap-shooting at running targets, such as jackrabbit, cottontail or squirrel.

Another very good reticle is the flat topped tapered post and crosshair. This is perhaps the best of the lot for extremely poor light conditions, showing up against the gloom of late evening or early morning. It is very good for jump-shooting rabbits, taking snapshots at squirrels, and in big game shooting as well. But it is not a good choice for long range sniping because it covers too much target at extended ranges.

One virtue of post and crosshair, or post alone, shouldn't be overlooked by small game hunters. A post and crosshair has very much the appearance of a receiver sight with a square gold bead front sight. This build-up gives a hunter a feeling of familiarity, and a consequent transference of shooting skills from the one type sight to the other. To that extent it is conducive to acquiring a wide spread of field shooting ability, which is all to the good.

My two choices of reticles in scopes for small and large game shooting are crosshairs, and post and crosshair. I find these two types fitting in a large percentage of field shooting situations.

If a hunter avoids extremes, any reticle presently available as standard equipment on scopes will serve admirably in the small game field.

Windage and elevation adjustment in all good hunting scopes are precise, easily read in minutes of angle. Each click, or division of movement should give not more than a minute of angle change of impact.

Quality in scope sights comes relatively high. The best scopes of domestic manufacture cost from $40 to $100 dollars.

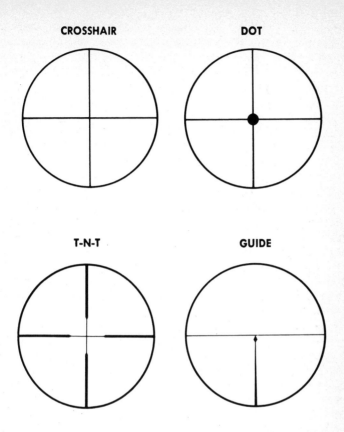

CROSSHAIR   **DOT**

T-N-T   **GUIDE**

(Courtesy Rolfe C. Spinning, Inc.)

Popular reticles in the Williams scope line. The T-N-T stands for "thick and thin" and this type is second in popularity to their standard crosshair reticle. The Guide reticle claims advantages in poor light and when there is only the shortest time for getting off a fast aimed shot. The dot at center of the Dot reticle covers 3 inches at 100 yards in 4X.

They are exemplified by such brand names as Lyman Wolverine, Lyman Alaskan, Norman-Ford Texan, Fecker Commando, Weaver, Series 60, Unertl Hawk and Leopold Pioneer. Cheap scopes are not bargains at any price!

A beautiful series of rifle scopes, designed in Pasadena, California are being made in Japan and imported under strin-

The Bushnell 4X Custom model made for .22's.

gent specifications of the Bushnell Optical Corporation. These scopes will compare favorably with the best of our domestic brand scopes in quality, and they are sold at modest prices. Of six different brands of scopes tested during the small and big game seasons, fair weather and foul, Leopold Pioneer, Norman-Ford Texan, and Bushnell's line of hunting scopes came through without fault.

TELESCOPE SIGHT MOUNTS

A scope sight is only as good as its mount. Unless you have a mount with all the refinements the best craftsmen bring to the problem of wedding scope and rifle, you will not realize the high accuracy potential of which both you and your rifle are capable. Generally speaking, both scopes and mounts are poor compromises if they are specifically designed for target shooting, then perforce, are used for all small game shooting. Not only are they wrong mechanically for field use, they also are wrong aesthetically as well. A hunter's rifle should have machine beauty complementing its utilitarian purpose.

As you approach the problem of hunting scopes and mounts from the standpoint of small game shooting, without trying to adapt target scopes and mounts, both aesthetic and utilitarian purposes are nicely met. Consider the beauty of a Texan 6X scope and Redfield mount or a Bushnell 8X Scope-chief and a Williams mount. These scopes and mounts appear as an integral part of the rifle. They are beautifully crafted and aesthetically pleasing. And that is important, even from the practical standpoint of accuracy. They look like they would shoot accurately.

In contrast, some of the out and out target scopes and

mounts often seen afield when woodchuck, coyote or ground squirrel is the quarry, look like an afterthought—something put on a rifle without design or reason. Windage and elevations adjustments are as homely by accident as they could possibly be made by design.

Most out and out target mounts have external adjustments for their scopes. But the problem of external adjustment for hunting scopes is much better solved in such splendid mounts as the Leopold, or the Jaeger side mounts with these features.

Small game hunters must be, above all, efficient, all-around field shots, if their skill is to be used later in big game hunting. Over-specialization of sighting equipment is scarcely a practical approach to shooting a limit of fox squirrel, or rolling a few cottontails.

There are two types of scope mounts, generally speaking: bridge type mounts and side mounts.

Side mounts deserve especial consideration by small game hunters using their off-season rifles to develop skill for those autumn forays in the north woods. A scope using side mounts can be taken off, or put on a rifle within seconds, complementing the iron sights, to get as great a spread of shooting accuracy as iron and scope sights give a woods rifleman.

At times during a severe snow or rainstorm, scope sights are practically useless for hunting. This must be taken into consideration. Side mounts are excellent for this exigency of field shooting, especially in the Williams, Jaeger, Sako and Pachmayr.

The Sako mount, like the Williams mount, is quickly detachable. In addition there is a Sako peep sight that may be substituted for the scope during severe, stormy weather when a scope sight may be canceled out. This Sako peep sight, once sighted in, may be carried in a hunting jacket for such emergencies.

In using an off-set mount for such rifles, there is the problem of having a stock which takes this off-set position into consideration. In mounting an off-set scope on my Model 71, Winchester 348, a beautiful squirrel and blue grouse rifle, when loaded with midrange charges and gas check lead bullets, I had a stock built special.

This stock was designed both for offset telescope and conventional iron sights. The cheekpiece was flattened just enough to give firm face support when using the off-set scope sight. To achieve this, the lower part of the cheekpiece was brought out full, while the top was cut away enough so that when the head is tilted slightly, iron sights are instantly available.

This rifle has been field-tested during the past two seasons, both on small game and in hunting elk. The specialized stocking has worked out wonderfully well, too. It would be pointless to give the dimension of this stock, designed for use of an off-set scope sight. The dimensions, other than the cheekpiece are conventional. The cheekpiece is the result of a great deal of "cut and try." The stock was beautifully crafted of "fiddleback" myrtle.

Another method of adapting off-set scope mounts to conventional stocks is to mount them on the side of the rifle a hunter normally shoots from—on the right side for a right handed shooter—the left side for a southpaw.

Off-set mounts, with iron sights, instantly available are becoming increasingly popular with hunters. One manufacturer of both off-set and bridge type mounts told me that 50 percent of their sales, regardless of the type of rifle, was for off-set scope mounts. This is especially true of the lever action and other top ejecting rifles.

Williams side mounts have some very practical, interesting features for the small game shooter. This mount is quickly detachable, being removed from the rifle by loosening only two lock nuts. Yet it returns to a very positive zero when replaced. In addition, this company supplies a receiver sight which is interchangable with the scope. This receiver sight, it seems to me, has two very distinct purposes. First and foremost is the fact that if an accident should occur to your scope, you have a sight with which it can be replaced in the field without the use of tools. The second place where this iron sight comes in very handy, even at the expense of reiteration, is for field conditions where scope sights are less than practical, such as stormy, extremely wet and foggy weather.

Jaeger side mounts are excellent choices for all rifles. They are especially attractive, in that like the Williams mount, they leave very little on the receiver of the rifle when the scope is removed. The attachment feature of the Jaeger is very much like that of the old Griffin and Howe side mounts. The Jaeger mounts also come in off-set for all top ejecting Winchester rifles. But, like the Echo, they are not adapted to all hunting scopes on these rifles. The Bushnell scopes cannot be mounted due to the lack of eye relief.

The Pachmayr low swing mount is very popular among experienced hunters. This scope swings aside for instant use of iron sights. In addition, it has a very easy detachable feature, enabling a hunter to remove it entirely when the exigency of field shooting calls for the use of iron sights. Pachmayr low swing mount also comes in off-set for top ejecting rifles. It is also adapted to all scopes, including the Bushnell.

The Williams off-set mount is an excellent choice for all calibers. Probably more thought went into designing this mount than in most presently available. It is designed, not only for top ejecting rifles, such as the Winchester lever action, Krag, and Model 8-81 Remingtons, but also for the Winchester Model 70 bolt action, Remington Model 721 and other side ejecting rifles, including the Marlin lever actions and Savage Model 99. A hunter desiring instant availability of iron sights, as well as a scope, may have it with the Williams off-set mount, regardless of the type of rifle he uses. It is easily detachable, leaving nothing to clutter the bridge of a rifle. But a trifle more base is left on the receiver than with the other side mounts under consideration.

The Willams off-set mount is a splendid combination in connection with Williams' Foolproof receiver sight, giving instant choice of iron or scope sights. It is adapted to all scopes presently available.

In addition to their off-set mounts, Williams also make a quick detachable, bridge type mount. A scope equipped with Williams rings is interchangeable between their two types of mounts. Williams bridge type mounts can be obtained with their Ace-In-the-Hole Peep sight, which fits the base of the mount when the scope is removed, very good field insurance, if you happen to be on an extended hunting trip with just one rifle available.

Another very good bridge type mount is the Redfield Junior. It is available for practically all small game rifles. My Marlin lever action .22, Model 39A, is equipped with this mount, complementing a Bushnell 2½ power Scopechief, for one of the best tree squirrel outfits I have ever had in my hands. The Redfield mounts give low, clean mounting without cluttering up the receiver; "Looking," as my old hunting friend Al Lyman once said, "like she growed there."

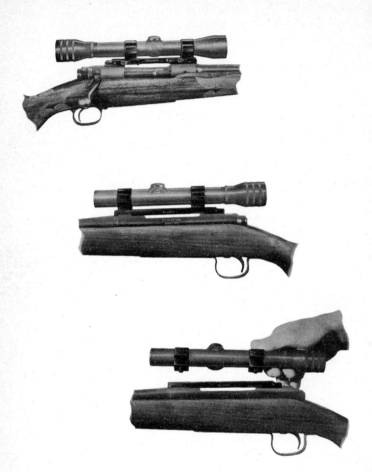

Illustrating the mounting and speedy detachable feature of one of the
Williams Quick Convertible bridge mounts.

Maynard P. Buehler makes another good bridge type mount which has been field tested over several small and big game seasons without finding any fault with it, on the bridge of a Model 70 Winchester .270. It has an iron peep sight which can be used on the mount when the scope is removed.

There are other scope mounts available, some of them very good. But the mounts which have been under consideration here are those which I have personally taken afield, fair weather and foul. All of them came through excellently.

Bushnell's Custom-DM, complete with detachable mounts for use with standard bases.

CHAPTER 9

Sighting In A Small Game Rifle

There is a best sight setting for every rifle, from .22 rimfire to the wildest wild cat caliber, a range, once your sights are zeroed in, which gives you the best possible accuracy at all field distances. Careful study, plenty of shooting, and an intimate knowledge of exterior ballistics will give you the know-how to arrive at the best possible distance to zero your particular rifle.

Your sighting in is conditioned by the game you hunt, as well as by the caliber you use. Obviously, there is not as much leeway between a miss and a killing hit when the game is tree squirrel as there is in shooting larger game. The vital area of a squirrel is covered by about an inch and a half. Just a little miscalculation in sight setting, added to the natural errors of aim, can put you off your target, or worse yet, give only a crippling hit.

A .22 rifle, sighted in for tree squirrel hunting, using the .22 long rifle high speed hollow point ammunition is working with a 1365 fps velocity. This gives a bullet drop of 5.5 inches at one hundred yards, if you are sighted in to hit point of aim at 50 yards. Such sight settings would put you off the target at around 85 yards.

Tree squirrel shooting is a comparatively short range affair, with most of the shots being taken within 35 yards. So you wouldn't be greatly handicapped with your squirrel rifle zeroed in at 50 yards. But why not sight in for the maximum range, if it will not cancel out your careful holding on the shorter range shots?

Sighted to hit point of aim at 75 yards, your bullet would be about an inch above your line of sights at 25 yards. At 50 yards it would be a full 1½ inches above. At 100 yards it would be 3 inches low. Should you get a shot at this extreme range, and there will be some occasionally, the sure knowledge that you have 3 inches' drop of the bullet for which you must compensate, makes a hit relatively simple.

Ranges less than a 100 yards, with your rifle sighted in to hit point of aim at 75 yards, are even more easily estimated. Even if you make a mistake of 25 yards in your estimate, your sight setting at 75 yards will amply compensate for the error. For at best you cannot be off more than a few inches. The trajectory curve of a .22 long rifle highspeed, with your rifle sighted in for 75 yards, is relatively flat over a 100 yards range.

Let's trace the path of one of those shots in detail, give it woods application. Suppose it is a fox squirrel you have your sights on. The range, mind you, is not known. But from previous shooting it appears to be around 25 yards. Your rifle is sighted in to hit point of aim at 75 yards. You known that at 25 yards the bullet will strike about ½ inch high. That measurement of one inch, as seen through your scope sight, is about the width of a squirrel's head. If it is actually 25, as you estimated it, your crosshairs must be centered a fraction below his head for a killing hit assuming the head is your aiming point, as it should be at this range.

You carefully squeeze off the shot and tumble the squirrel, the point of impact being near the top of the head. But suppose you had made an error in estimating range. Suppose, that instead of being 25 yards, it is 35 yards. You are still in for a killing hit for the simple reason that you have selected the *best* range at which to zero your rifle, using .22 high-speed ammunition.

At 35 yards the bullet would be a bit higher, but still touching the head for a killing hit. At 20 yards with the same point of aim you would still be in, your bullet striking a bit lower than at 25 yards. You can readily see why, once your rifle is sighted in at its best range, there is no reason in tryng to estimate your distances in yards. It is much better to simplify your shooting into *short range, medium range* and *long range*, having only three measurements with which to estimate shots.

Applying this to your .22 rifle, the target that fox squirrel offered in a beechnut at 25 yards, you made a short range shot. The bullet is not at its maximum trajectory height at the target. A medium range shot would be from 40 to 60 yards the points between which the bullet hasn't left the line of sights by more than 1½ inches. From here on out past the distance at which you zeroed your rifle to the point beyond which you couldn't expect a clean kill, even though your holding was perfect, is your long range bracket. In case of targets as small as squirrel, expert shots would place this at 100 yards.

Applying this same system to your big game rifle, when using midrange handloads for off-season shooting, one comes up with a lot of interesting, worthwhile data. This is

Here is where you start. All rifles for large or small game should be carefully sighted in at their best range. For small game this means that the bullet cannot be more than 1.5" above or below point of aim at any effective range for tree squirrel and some ground squirrel shooting. For most other shooting, the bullet can be as much as 2.5" above or below point of aim and still be effective. Consult the cartridge ballistic charts and trajectary data obtainable free from cartridge manufacturers.

not only beneficial in your small game hunting, but has a pay-off also when you are elk or deer hunting.

Take my own heavy caliber, the now obsolete .348 Winchester Model 71. Here, with proper handloads, is an excellent squirrel and rabbit caliber. It has just the proper amount of weight for steady holding, and is very accurate with midrange loads. Only difference between shooting deer or elk with it, and using it on tree squirrel is that the squirrels are the more difficult targets. Of course, sight setting for those midrange, gas check loadings is different.

My midrange squirrel loading, taken from Lyman's Ideal Handbook, is as follows: 190 grain gas check bullet, 20 grains of 4759 Du Pont powder, giving me a velocity of 1400 feet a second.

With that velocity figure, I sight this load in to hit point of aim at 75 yards to get maximum coverage at all squirrel and rabbit ranges. Sighted in at this distance, the bullet flight above or below line of sight is about as follows: 25 yards, one inch above line of sight; 50 yards, 1¼ above; on at 75 yards; and 100 yards, 3½ inches below point of aim.

The trajectory curve of this 190 grain gas check is not so great but what you can take head shots out to a full 50 yards —if you remember the point of aim necessary for each easily estimated distance: short, medium, and long range shots.

When you step out of the woods, a sniping rifle in your hands, long range shooting with ground squirrel or woodchuck on your mind, you still have the same yardstick of measurements for your range estimating: short, medium, long. But you are playing in the big league now. Different calibers and velocities make a short range shot something else than those obtained with a .22 rimfire. Your rifle must be sighted differently to take full advantage of its ranging potential.

My Sako .222 caliber has plenty on the ball, and must be sighted in carefully to take advantage of its superb accuracy and ranging ability.

The range table out to the practical limits of its effectiveness on such game as woodchuck and ground squirrel, using a 50 grain bullet is as follows, sighted to hit point of aim at 200 yards: at 25 yards the bullet is 0.5 above line of sights at 50 yards; 2.5 above at 100 yards; on point of aim at 200; and about 4.5 inches below at 250 yards.

Sighted to hit point of aim at 200 yards, a short range shot with my .222 is any distance out to 100 yards. You can hold directly on any of the ordinary sniping targets such as woodchuck or ground squirrel. From 100 to 200 yards would be in the medium range bracket, with your holding still on your point of intended impact. From here out to 250 yards would be in the long range bracket, with some holding-over indicated.

Properly sighted in at 200 yards, you could be as much as 50 yards off in your estimating of range and still make a killing hit at all practical field ranges with this caliber. And for the simple reason that your sighting takes full advantage of this splendid flat shooting .222 caliber.

The same things may be said of the many wildcat calibers. Divide their practical range up into *three* easily estimated distances. Apply this to their trajectory curve; sight in to keep bullet drop within the limits of your intended target size, and about 90 percent of your unaccountable misses are compensated for, especially in the medium and long range brackets.

It holds good for big game shooting. It holds good for small game plinking—long range sniping. Any type of field rifle shooting will benefit by this simplification of range estimation, and proper sight setting.

The actual mechanics of sighting in a rifle are well known to most hunters. You know that a minute of angle, for all practical purposes, is about one inch for each hundred yards of range. If you are sighting in a rifle with receiver sight calibrated in one-half minutes of angle, as most of the better grade sights are, each click of elevation or windage moves your center of impact at 100 yards a half inch, two clicks for each inch of movement. Most scope sights are also calibrated in one-half minutes of angle.

Usually, after mounting scope or receiver sights, the simplest procedure to get on the target is to boresight your rifle. This, stripped of its esoteric nonsense, means that you bring your sights and the bore of your rifle into adjustment by sighting through the bore, and centering it directly on your target, usually at one hundred yards. Then the sights are brought into adjustment on the same aiming point.

To do this properly you must rest your rifle on two sandbags, or in a cradle, made by cutting two V notches in a box to form a stable rest for your rifle. The bolt, of course, is removed for bore sighting, and in the case of lever action rifles,

Rimfire Rifle Cartridges

Cartridge	Bullet Wt. Grs.	Type	Velocity (fps) Muzzle	100 yds.	Energy (ft. lbs.) Muzzle	100 yds.	Mid-Range Trajectory (Inches) 100 yds.
22 Short Super-X	29	L, K‡	1125	920	81	54	4.3
22 Short H.P. Super-X	27	L, K‡	1155	920	80	51	4.2
22 Long Super-X	29	L, K‡	1240	965	99	60	3.8
22 Long Rifle Super-X	40	L, K‡	1285	1025	147	93	3.4
22 Long Rifle H.P. Super-X	37	L, K‡	1315	1020	142	85	3.4
22 Long Rifle Shot Super-X	— #12 Shot —						
22 WRF (22 Rem. Spl.) Super-X (inside lubricated)	45	L, K	1450	1110	210	123	2.7
22 Winchester Magnum Rim Fire Super-X	40	JHP	2000	1390	355	170	1.6
22 Winchester Magnum Rim Fire Super-X	40	FMC	2000	1390	355	170	1.6
22 Short T22	29	Lead*	1045	—	70	—	5.6
22 Long Rifle T22	40	Lead*	1145	975	116	84	4.0
22 Long Rifle Super-Match Mark III and Improved L.V. EZXS	40	Lead*	1120	950	111	80	4.2
22 Short Kant-Splash and Spatterpruf (Gallery Pack)	29	Disinteg.*	1045	—	70	—	—
22 Short Super Kant-Splash and Super Spatterpruf (Gallery Pack)	15	Disinteg.*	1810	—	109	—	—
22 Winchester Automatic (inside lubricated)	45	L, K	1055	930	111	86	4.6

FMC—Full Metal Case   ‡—Wax Coated   *—Lubricated   L—Lubaloy   JHP—Jacketed Hollow Point   K—Kopperklad

(From 1972 Winchester-Western catalog.)

a Borescope must be used in order to see through the barrel.

You get nothing more than an approximation of your actual bullet impact by bore sighting. But it does help to get on the paper with that first shot.

Barrel vibration, differences in holding and all intangibles of rifle shooting make each rifle and loading a bit different. What you are actually doing when you sight in a rifle to its final accuracy after bore sighting, is to bring your sight into relationship with the bore under the stress of firing. It is alive then and very sensitive, responsive to the least change of ammunition, powder charge, bullet weight. Once you are on the target bore sighting, the final adjustments of sights must be made with live ammunition.

Of course you know that you move your rear sight setting in the same direction you want to move your grouping. If you are out to the right of your aiming point, or at three o'clock, you naturally click on the proper amount of left windage to move your center of impact in to your point of aim. If you are shooting low, the correction is made by moving your sight up, giving it more elevation.

In sighting in a rifle for field shooting, the center of impact and point of aim should be the same for the range selected. That gives you a reference point for those subdivisions of field ranges: your bullet being slighly above point of aim at the short ranges, on at medium distances, and slightly below at the longer ranges.

Each rifle, even at the expense of reiteration, must be sighted in at its own best distance to cover its maximum range latitude most efficiently; all the rest is routine.

Sighting in, however, is a job which you must do yourself, for no two hunters ever see their sights the same. They hold their rifles differently. These peculiarities of eyesight and holding causes rifles to group differently—enough so that you could very easily miss a squirrel's head when your target is half concealed in the multicolored autumn leaves of an oak.

PART IV

Small Game Hunting with Handguns

CHAPTER 10

Handguns For Small Game Hunting

It was the end of the trail. Before us the wilderness stretched toward the headwaters of Pistol River in Southwestern Oregon. Across the divide, you could, by traveling the rugged back country, eventually drop into the Rogue River drainage. But it was plenty rugged going. What we had in mind was fishing, hiking, exploring—being in the back country because it was back country, beautiful and unspoiled.

The fishing was good, too good. We took all the trout we needed, fishing the rise late evenings for a half hour. Squirrel hunting was also good, both red and gray squirrel. We hunted them with a Smith and Wesson K-22, and a .22 automatic Ruger.

Ever eat squirrel done to a turn over a small campfire, a good trout stream singing on the riffles below your trail camp, the first evening stars held captive in the dark pools? If you don't know, you don't know, that is all. If you do know, you understand the necessity of having a handgun when roaming the backcountry. On such trips, either fishing, hiking or exploring, a handgun should be standard equipment.

It is light to carry when weight must be considered. It is efficient for all small game hunting within reasonable range limits. Tree squirrels are made to order for a handgun—if the same amount of skill ordinarily used in shooting a rifle is brought to the problem of tumbling one from the hardwoods.

First question usually asked by hunters planning on adding a handgun to their kits is, what caliber is best for all-around small game field performance? It is an important question, too

—equally important with the problem of selecting proper rifles for small game hunting, and like the problem of selecting a rifle it has several answers.

A hunter's first handgun should be a .22 revolver or automatic pistol. When one starts with heavy caliber revolvers or pistols, such as the .45 Colt Auto, the .357 Smith and Wesson Magnum, or the .44 Special, the problem of accurate shooting is emphasized by the heavy recoil. Quite often the beginner will find himself developing a tendency to flinch, to get off sloppy, inaccurate shots because the big bores are a bit beyond his ability as yet.

A .22 handgun will cure this tendency by its mild report and its lack of recoil. In addition it will come closer to exemplifying the inherent accuracy of *all* well made handguns at a time when a beginner needs to discover that there is superb accuracy and ranging ability in all handguns.

A very good selection for the beginner is the Smith and Wesson K-.22. This .22 revolver, with its six inch barrel, excellent adjustable sights, and beautiful crisp trigger pull, is about tops for small game field shooting. It is not only a good field gun in its own right, it is also an excellent understudy for the larger calibers, such as the K-.38, .38/44 Outdoorsman, Smith and Wesson Model 44 target, or the .357 Magnum. The K-.22 weighs in at 38 ounces, plenty of weight for good steady holding.

Smith and Wesson .22 Kit Gun is also an ideal choice for back country hiking and fishing trips. It is compact, and light in weight, but with excellent field accuracy. This little revolver, with a barrel length of 4 inches weighs just 21 ounces. It can be dropped into an outside pocket of your rucksack, along with one hundred rounds of .22 long rifle hollow point ammunition, and the weight will scarcely be noticeable. Then, should you decide to do some pot hunting to supplement your pack grub, you have a very excellent choice for the job.

Many wilderness trappers of my acquaintance carry the Smith and Wesson Kit Gun on their trap lines, an excellent endorsement for reliability and accuracy. It is surprising the amount of game they take with it, in addition to shooting the larger trapped animals, such as raccoon, bobcat, and coyote.

Colt's Officers Model in .22 long rifle caliber is another very good small game handgun. It weighs 31 ounces with a 4½ inch barrel. It also has those all important adjustable sights. Just about anything said about the Smith and Wesson K-.22 is applicable to this handgun.

The Ruger Single Six is the quality single action .22 revolver for outdoorsmen. This revolver was brought about by popular demand. It is a very close copy of the fabulous Colt single action Frontier. The refinements which have been embodied in it, such as coiled mainspring and a bit faster lock time, are all to the good. But the traditional trappings of the much loved single action are all there, from grip to the distinct clicks when you thumb back the generous hammer. The Ruger Single Six comes with a five inch barrel and weights 36 ounches, trail side. It has semi-adjustable sights, and accuracy comparable with any of the quality revolvers.

Dropping down the line in price, an outdoorsman has a fairly wide choice of inexpensive revolvers from which to choose. Probably the best of the lot from the standpoint of accuracy and reliability are the Iver Johnson revolvers. I have carried an Iver Johnson sealed eight, Model 68 on a trap-line and in my rucksack while hunting, fishing and tramping the back country for several years and always it has proved reliable and accurate on both game and plinking targets.

Usually the inexpensive revolvers come from the factory with the trigger pulls which leave much to be desired. But a little time spent with a good oilstone can take the creep and unevenness out of them. If you haven't any ability at this, it is best to turn over the job to a gunsmith. Once the trigger pull is corrected, an Iver Johnson, or Champion .22 Target, the Super Shot, or the Harrington and Richardson Sportsman are all nice packsacks guns for the rough and tumble of hiking, hunting and plinking.

The .22 automatic pistols are well represented by three outstanding selections: Ruger, Hi-Standard and Colt. All these are good choices for the give and take of small game hunting. They are amply accurate enoug to snip the head off a grouse at twenty yards, knock off a tree squirrel, or roll a rabbit at reasonable range. Weights in these models range from 31 to 38 ounches. Barrel lengths are from 4½ to 6 inches.

It is just as natural for a woodsman to have preferences in handguns as it is for squirrels to climb trees.

My own preference in automatic .22 pistols is the Ruger. I carry this handgun a lot on my field trips. I have shot it over a period of two seasons, and more and more, I find myself

Browning Challenger .22 semiautomatic pistol.

Ruger Mark I .22 semiautomatic pistol—one of my favorites.

dropping it into my packsack when I am preparing for a wilderness trip. If you were to ask me why, the answer would be hard to come by. There are a lot of intangibles built into *all* firearms—little nuances of mechanical differences which add up to an over-all preference.

First off, I like the big, hand filling grip of this pistol. I like the angle at which it is set to the receiver. There is a natural pointing to the Ruger .22 automatic which spells good field shooting accuracy. I have yet to examine a Ruger which left the factory with a poor trigger pull, something which I cannot say about many handguns, with the exception of the Smith and Wesson, and Sturm-Ruger products.

All .22 handguns must be used with a great deal of judgment in small game hunting. A handgun, remember, is only a substitute for a rifle. It is limited in range and accuracy. A .22 handgun can be used for tree squirrel hunting, if you are careful to take only shots which offer a reasonable chance of killing. Eventually you will want something heavier for your small game handgun hunting. These heavier caliber handguns are the logical outgrowth of plenty of .22 handgun shooting. When an outdoorsman is ready for larger caliber handguns, he should be able to handle a .22 very accurately afield. By this time he will have decided preferences as to type of sights required for small game hunting. He will have preferences as to barrel length, and trigger pull. In short, plenty of .22 handgun shooting will develop skills which can be complemented and enlarged by going to heavier handguns.

Smith and Wsson revolvers, in their K series, enable a hunter to progressively up the power of his handguns without any radical change in design, weight, trigger pull or barrel length.

One of the best of the heavier calibers is the K-38 Smith and Wesson, in .38 Special caliber. It has superb accuracy and plenty of killing power for all small game shooting. In addition, the recoil is not the least bit unpleasant for a handgunner who has had plenty of shooting with a .22 revolver.

Killing power, of course, is a relative thing. I recall a hunting partner taking a black bear with a K-.38, using a 158 grain bullet at a velocity of 900 feet a second handload. Compared with a rifle, even those considered a bit on the underpowered side for deer, this loading is a pip-squeak, but with careful, accurate shooting, it kept this skilled woodsman from getting into some very serious trouble.

This bear, having been wounded by other hunters, was a bit cross-grained when my woodsman friend almost stepped on her. She was lying in an elk wallow near a forest trail at the time. She came to her feet, clicking her teeth together, and moving at an awkward lope toward him. All the while he was frantically unslinging his rucksack and clawing his .38 Special out of a side pocket. He dropped her neatly, though, with a head shot at fifteen feet. With careful, short range shooting, the .38 Special, K-.38 is a good killer.

I know several hunters who use this caliber for shooting treed game. It will tumble raccoon or bobcat from a tree, and in the hands of an experienced and accurate field shot, it will kill treed mountain lion or bear without trouble. Its best field, however, is in small game hunting, such as squirrel, rabbit and woodchuck, when a hunter wants to put plenty of stalking ability into his hunt in order to get within handgun range of such game.

Another very good choice in heavy handguns is the .38/44 Smith and Wesson, or the Colt Official Police in this caliber. Both these guns use the full line of .38 Special cartridges, and in addition they handle the .38 Special high speed loadings. This later loading is a souped up version of the standard .38 Special, driving a 150 grain bullet at 1100 feet a second, and with a muzzle energy of 400 foot pounds. By careful handloading, this caliber will drive this same bullet at 1250 feet a second with perfect safety, making it a superb cartridge for the larger treed game.

The Smith and Wesson Outdoorsman Target revolver in .38/44 caliber comes with splendid adjustable sights, 6 inch barrel and weighs 41¾ ounces. The Colt, Official Police in .38/44 caliber also comes with a 6 inch barrel, the preferred length for all handgun field shooting, semi-adjustable sights, and weighs 36 ounces. This weight is a bit on the light side for a revolver using as powerful load as the .38 Special High Speed, and for that reason most handgunners will find the Smith and Wesson, with its weight of 41¾ ounces more comfortable for field shooting.

The .357 and the .44 Magnums are the most powerful factory loading presently available. A revolver using either of these cartridges is an especially attractive one when you are prowling the backcountry, fishing, hiking and camping. The .357 Magnum gives you maximum power for self defense, using a 158 grain bullet at a velocity of 1450, with a muzzle energy of 690 foot pounds. In addition, it will handle any of the loads designed for the .38 Special, or the .38/44, giving you a wide range of cartridges from which to select.

Smith and Wesson's offering in .357 Magnum caliber comes with adjustable sights, and in barrel length from 3½ to 8¾ inches. It weighs 47 ounces with the longer length barrel. The Colt in this caliber comes with adjustable sights and barrel lengths of 4, 5, and 6 inches; it weighs about 43 ounces.

There are factors an outdoorsman should take into consideration in selecting a .357 Magnum for exclusive use with maximum loadings. Unless he is a very experienced revolver shot, it is doubtful if he will get his best accuracy with a .357 Magnum, using full powered loads. No one can step directly from a .22 handgun to a .357 Magnum. He should progress through the intermediate calibers, gradually developing his ability to handle recoil.

Of course the .357 Magnum, like any of the large caliber handguns, can be tamed with mid-range handloads, and by the use of .38 Special loadings. The power of these loadings can be stepped up as the hunter becomes more used to the peculiarities of his handgun, and when he feels he can use the extra power the heavier loads give him. But the .38 Special loads in the .357 Magnum will be found sufficiently powerful and superbly accurate for most small game shooting.

Some very extravagant claims are often made for the .357 Magnum handgun. Comparing the .357 Magnum to such rifles as the .30/30 is nonsense. The .357 drives a 158 grain bullet at 1450 feet a second in the maximum loadings. It has a muzzle energy of 690 pounds. The .30/30, a questionable deer caliber, with a muzzle velocity of 2200 feet a second, has a muzzle energy of 1860 foot pounds, using a 170 grain bullet, almost three time the striking power of the .357 Magnum in its best loading.

All handguns are comparatively short range. A hunter should confine his small game shooting to not more than sixty yards, thirty-five is much better. In many ways this constitutes a virtue, in that it places emphasis on painstaking stalking to get within efficient handgun range.

The spread of handgun shooting ranges from the .22 to .44 Smith and Wesson is not nearly as great as the comparable range spread of suitable small game rifles. You have enough accuracy and power with a .22 handgun to take rabbit and squirrel, using hollow-point high speed ammunition, to about thirty-five yards. When you switch to heavier caliber handguns you will not up your sure killing range much beyond the before mentioned sixty yards.

The .44 Magnum Smith and Wesson is the choice of many backwoodsmen carrying a heavy revolver for self protection as well as small game shooting. It has many advantages, when measured from the standpoint of practical field use, too. This caliber drives a 246 grain bullet at a modest velocity of 770 feet a second in its factory loadings. But with handloads, the .44 Special will drive a 250 grain Keith bullet at 1200 feet a second, a velocity close to that of the .357 Magnum, and with a much heavier bullet.

Many outdoorsmen believe that this is our most accurate handgun. It surely is the easiest for which to handload, giving nail driving accuracy with a long list of handloads from the midrange to full powered loadings.

The .44 Special Smith and Wesson in their Model 44 Target weighs 39½ ounces, has a 6½ inch barrel, and comes with adjustable sights. It is an excellent "tree" gun when you are running heavy game with dogs, in addition to being deadly on small game with proper loading.

There are many other calibers which might be considered, but this spread of handguns just about covers all the *best* when measured against small game hunting requirements.

Sight requirements for small game handguns are not essentially different from those selected for small game rifles, in one sense of the word. You have the problem of dim light in the woods, or neutral colored targets, all of which adds up to a front sight which gives plenty of contrast to make it stand out against the target. This is best accomplished by either a square white Patridge type sight, or a square gold bead, such as the Redfield Sourdough, which can be adapted to handgun use by installing a ramp base for it. A red plastic bead is also good, though it has a tendency to blend with the background late in the evening.

Present-day handguns are almost all adapted to special scope sights. These are very attractive where a hunter is using a handgun for small game hunting. They are, of course, very slow from the standpoint of getting off a quick shot at running small game, such as squirrel or rabbit. But the use of scopes on handguns does give an extra element of precision, when compared to iron sights.

Front sights with rounded beads are very poor selections. Like comparable rifle sights, they have a tendency to shoot away from the light source. When the sun is directly overhead, they shoot low. When the light is from the left, there is a tendency to shoot to the right of your target, all because the gunner centers the brightest part of his front sight bead in the rear sight notch.

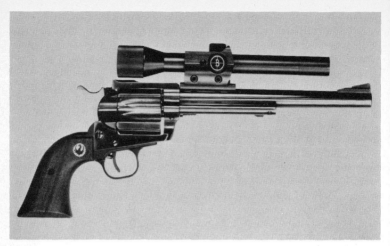

Bushnell 2.6X Phantom scope on Ruger Hawkeye revolver.

Bushnell scope on heavy Colt revolver.

Rear sights should be adjustable, both for windage and elevation. Those with a square notch are best for either target or game shooting.

The problem of carrying a handgun appears relatively simple to the inexperienced hunter. Just buy a good belt holster, swing your handgun to your belt and you are all ready. All ready for what? The most uncomfortable day afield you ever put in.

Swing a 41 ounce weight from your belt for a full eight hours afield and you are going to be plenty tired of the deal before you finish your hunt. It will swing and bump your leg. It will pull down unmercifully. By noon you will ponder the pleasure of leaving it beside the trail.

Best solution is a shoulder rig which will enable you to carry it under your left arm, the weight coming directly on the shoulder where it is scarcely noticeable. With a proper shoulder rig, you can wear your gun while carrying a rucksack.

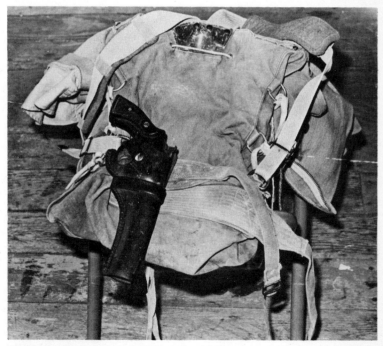

Rucksack, handgun and holster—a kit of just the essentials kept ready to go, fast to don when the chance for a trip into the woods comes up.

Showing where the handgun is worn on the bellyband of the rucksack; considerable weight is thus taken off the belt and transferred to the shoulder.
Some woodsmen, including myself, often carry the handgun in the rucksack.

However, I have found it much more to the point to detach the shoulder rig when packing, and drop the gun in an outside pocket of my rucksack. In states where this would constitute a concealed weapon, it is a simple matter to attach it to the side of the pack with a snap and thong.

In selecting a holster for a handgun, one can easily come a cropper, too. There are many holsters on the market which had their inspiration in those worn by drugstore cowboys and Hollywood gun slingers, all nicely cut away for a quick draw, all nicely designed to drop a valuable gun on the rocks the minute you stoop over.

Just forget the quick draw, and all the Western trappings associated with revolvers. Get a holster which is opened at the barrel-end so that wet leaves and water will not collect in it to rust your gun. See that there is a snap across the trigger guard to keep your gun secure. You are not going to break any speed records getting into action, but that is unimportant. The important thing is what you do after getting into action with a handgun.

Remember you are carrying a substitute for a rifle, once it is out of its holster you have the problem of shooting it accurately, or there is little point in carrying it afield.

Center-fire Pistol and Revolver Cartridges

Cartridge	Wt. Grs.	Bullet Type	Barrel Length	Muzzle Velocity (fps)	Muzzle Energy (ft. lbs.)
25 Automatic (6.35mm) (Oilproof)	50	FMC	2"	810	73
*256 Winchester Magnum Super-X	60	OPE	8½"	2350	735
30 Luger (7.65mm) (Oilproof)	93	FMC	4½"	1220	305
32 Automatic (Oilproof)	71	FMC	4"	905	130
32 Smith & Wesson (Oilproof) (inside lubricated)	85	L, Lead	3"	680	90
32 Smith & Wesson Long (Oilproof) (inside lubricated)	98	L, Lead	4"	705	115
*32 Short Colt (Oilproof) Greased	80	Lubaloy	4"	745	100
*32 Long Colt (Oilproof) (inside lubricated)	82	Lubaloy	4"	755	105
†32 Colt New Police (Oilproof) (inside lubricated)	98	Lead	4"	680	100
32-20 Winchester (Oilproof) (inside lubricated)	100	L, Lead	6"	1030	235
32-20 Winchester (Oilproof)	100	SP	6"	1030	235
*357 Magnum Jacketed Hollow Point Super-X (Oilproof)	110	JHP	8⅜"	1410	—
*357 Magnum Super-X (Oilproof) (inside lubricated)	158	Lubaloy	8⅜"	1410	695
*357 Magnum Metal Piercing Super-X (Oilproof) (inside lubricated, lead bearing)	158	Met. Pierc.	8⅜"	1410	695
*357 Magnum Jacketed Hollow Point Super-X (Oilproof)	158	JHP	8⅜"	1450	740
*357 Magnum Jacketed Soft Point Super-X (Oilproof)	158	JSP	8⅜"	1450	740
†9mm Luger (Parabellum) (Oilproof)	115	FMC	4"	1140	330
†9mm Luger (Parabellum) (Oilproof)	100	PP	4"	1325	390
38 Smith & Wesson (Oilproof) (inside lubricated)	145	L, Lead	4"	685	150
38 Special (Oilproof) (inside lubricated)	158	L, Lead	6"	855	255
38 Special (Oilproof) (inside lubricated, lead bearing)	158	Met. Pt.	6"	855	255
†38 Special (MS) Police	158	Lead, HP	6"	1060	395
38 Special Super Police (Oilproof) (inside lubricated)	200	L, Lead	6"	730	235
†38 Special Semi Wad Cutter Super-Speed (Oilproof) (inside lubricated)	158	Lead	6"	1060	395
*38 Special Super-X (Oilproof) (inside lubricated)	150	Lubaloy	6"	1060	375
*38 Special Metal Piercing Super-X (Oilproof) (inside lubricated, lead bearing)	150	Met. Pierc.	6"	1060	375
38 Special Super-Match and Match Mid-Range Clean Cutting (Oilproof) (inside lubricated)	148	Lead	6"	770	195
*38 Special Super-Match (Oilproof) (inside lubricated)	158	Lead	6"	855	255
*38 Short Colt (Oilproof) Greased	130	Lubaloy	6"	730	150
*38 Long Colt (Oilproof) (inside lubricated)	150	Lubaloy	6"	730	175
38 Automatic Super-X and Super-Speed (For use only in 38 Colt Super and Colt Commander Automatic Pistols)	130	FMC	5"	1280	475
38 Automatic (Oilproof) (For all 38 Automatic Pistols)	130	FMC	4½"	1040	310
380 Automatic (Oilproof)	95	FMC	3¾"	955	190
38-40 Winchester (Oilproof)	180	SP	5"	975	380
*44 Smith & Wesson Special (Oilproof) (inside lubricated)	246	Lead	6½"	755	310
*44 Magnum Super-X (Gas Check)	240	Lubaloy	6½"	1470	1150
44-40 Winchester (Oilproof)	200	SP	7½"	975	420
45 Colt (Oilproof) (inside lubricated)	255	L, Lead	5½"	880	410
45 Automatic (Oilproof)	230	FMC	5"	850	370
*45 Automatic Super-Match Clean Cutting	185	FMC	5"	775	245

*— Western Brand Only
†— Winchester Brand Only
Met. Pierc.— Metal Piercing
FMC— Full Metal Case
SP— Soft Point
L— Lubaloy
JHP— Jacketed Hollow Point
JSP— Jacketed Soft Point
Met. Pt.— Metal Point
OPE— Open Point Expanding
HP— Hollow Point
PP— Power Point

CHAPTER 11

Small Game Shooting With Handguns

East of my cabin the hills rise fold on fold, a mixed forest of firs, and hemlock, with hazel and huckleberry on the open ridges. It is a boss setup for squirrel in autumn. Before you come to these ridges, however, you will cross my not too well cared for upland pastures, a patchwork of grass and clover, thickets of berry vines. It all adds up to some very good small game hunting. I hunt squirrel in the woods with a Model 39-A .22 lever action Marlin. At times I stillhunt rabbit through those overgrown pastures. But always, when the season shows I have harvested the surplus, I turn to handgun hunting through those briar grown pastures and along those high ridges.

Sure, I take less game hunting with a handgun. I also put in more time in careful stalking, re-emphasizing the importance of woodcraft in all hunting. Later, when I prowl those same ridges with a big game rifle in my hands, I am actually aware of the important part handgun hunting plays in making me a more efficient big game shot and hunter.

In handgun shooting afield you have every rifle problem of steady holding, trigger squeeze, and trajectory doubly emphasized. Once you become an accurate field shot with a handgun, rifle shooting will seem startlingly easy in comparison.

There are two approaches to handgun field shooting, just as there are two approaches to field shooting with a rifle. You can adapt target range techniques to field requirements with either. Or you can subordinate target shooting techniques to field requirements with greatly increased efficiency in your game shooting.

If there was ever a sport handicapped with a lot of useless trappings, it is that of handgun shooting. A stylized method of handling handguns, more in keeping with dueling, has been the bane of handguns for years. Maybe this is because it started out as a "gentleman's weapon" when it was considered smart for a couple of knotheads to get up at dawn and take a few cracks at each other at thirty paces—off-hand, of course.

They missed each other more often than not, and a lot of sportsmen are still missing with handguns because they still use a dueling approach to the problem of shooting.

Consider a difficult shot with either a rifle or handgun. Suppose you have in mind a fox squirrel, tree top high, in an autumn touched walnut or oak. A rifleman will take every advantage afforded by any natural rest in his shooting. He will use a steady sitting position if possible, resting his hand against a tree—anything to squeeze an extra fraction of an inch accuracy from his shooting. But how about the average handgun shooter confronted with the same problem? More than likely he will up and blaze away at his target without any advantage of rest, dueling fashion, and with about the usual dueling results.

Honestly now, can you think of any reason why a handgunner shouldn't also take full advantage of a steady position for his shooting, just as a rifleman does? Only recently the army took a long searching look at its program of pistol training. It measured it against the demands of battle shooting. As a result, there has been a drastic revision of training positions, something which should have happened several decades ago.

Today the army teaches soldiers to shoot with a handgun from the *sitting, kneeling,* and *prone* positions, in addition to the standing off-hand position. In this they are merely taking a leaf from the backwoods trapper and hunter, who have always used handguns for field shooting in this manner.

Accuracy is increased by at least seventy-five percent, using practical rifle techniques, "woods holding" a handgun.

If you can keep your shots in a six-inch circle at twenty-five yards off-hand, and it is surprising how many outdoorsmen cannot, you will be able to keep them in two inches from the sitting position. If you can keep them in three inches off-hand, you will literally stack them one on top of the other, "woods holding" your handgun, taking every advantage of position the shot affords.

The most practical field position for handgun shooting, especially for open country where the target is either rabbit, ground squirrel or woodchuck, is the sitting position. You can hold handguns rock steady for those comparatively long range shots of fifty yards or so, driving a bullet with startling accuracy, when measured against the conventional off-hand revolver stance.

Once, hiking through the back country with Al Lyman, I watched him perform on a variety of small game with a .38 Special Smith and Wesson. During our four day hike he took three rabbits, a grey squirrel and a blue grouse to supplement our rather light grubstake.

Hunters using a handgun to shoot game birds should first consult the state game laws on this. In some states and provinces it is accepted practice. In others it is forbidden.

The grouse I especially remember because it was such a beautiful shot, fully exemplifying the high accuracy potential of handgun shooting. We topped out on an open timbered ridge where the small fir stood as straight as Coldstream Guards. Scattered through the open glades, clumps of huckleberry bushes bowed under a heavy weight of rich black fruit. Raccoon had been feeding on them along with a few bear and occasional blue grouse.

The particular blue grouse I have in mind flew from a clump of huckleberry to perch well out on the bare lower limbs of a slender fir, a shot of about thirty-five yards. Al dropped into the sitting position, moved his feet slightly to get into a rock steady stance. At the sound of the shot the big blue grouse came tumbling from its perch to beat a tattoo on the forest floor with its wings. When I walked down to pick it up, I found its head neatly severed. A few hours later this grouse was simmering over our evening campfire.

What chance would a handgunner have, even the most expert, of taking that grouse using the stylized, dueling-target range off-hand shooting?

The sitting position is not greatly different with a handgun than the sitting position used in rifle shooting. Sit down, face your target, feet well apart, making a tripod support for your body. Grasp your handgun normally at the grip with your

Sitting position, using a handgun. Very accurate and utilized often when shooting for the pot.

right hand, assuming you are a right handed shooter, then place your left hand over your right, your elbows resting over your knees. There must be no tension in your position. It should be relaxed.

A little practice in this position will immediately give you much better field accuracy with a handgun than most of the expert off-hand target shooting handgunners attain. It's a long shot from the Western quick draw, beloved of story spinners, as well as dueling. Your hand will not be a blur of action as you snake your revolver from its holster, believe me. But there are other and more satisfying rewards. One of them is the aroma of small game stewing over your evening campfire when you are off on a hiking, exploring, or wilderness fishing trip.

Another very good field position is kneeling. This position is less steady than the sitting, just as it is in rifle shooting. But it is slightly faster. You can drop down on one knee as you

Kneeling position—productive of much more accuracy than the usual off-hand try (standing, but with no rest).

bring your handgun from its holster for a quick shot, getting into action faster when a split second, wedded to accuracy, may mean the difference between a shot and no shot at all.

I recall one day's hunt with a handgun when ground squirrel was my quarry. I used the kneeling position time after time to snap shots at squirrels when they stood erect, momentarily, before popping down their holes. This final conning of their territory before diving to safety had a time element attached to it that made handgun shooting from a kneeling position fit it like a glove. I dropped into a kneeling position, resting my elbow on my right knee, got off my shot with dispatch, or found myself staring at a vacant mound of dirt in front of a ground squirrel's burrow.

Ranges that day were around fifty yards. I was using a .38 Special Smith and Wesson, 158 grain gas check bullet in front of 5.8 grains of Unique powder, for a velocity of about 1000 feet a second, a killing load.

Variation of kneeling position when rest or support is available. Taking a
cut at a ground squirrel—head shot at about 35 yards.

Another position you will often see exemplified by backwoodsmen using a revolver is the *standing, tree-rest position*.
This is a very practical, steady position, and is especially useful
when you are shooting upward at an acute angle, when the
sitting or kneeling position is scarcely feasible. Stand up to a
small tree about six or eight inches in diameter, rest your gun
arm alongside it, your handgun well beyond the bole of the
tree. Now reach around the tree from the other side with
your free hand, grasp your gunhand at the wrist. Put a slight
pressure on it. Notice how those sights steady down on your
target?

When a big fox squirrel is at his antics in a beech tree,
pausing occasionally to shuck out a tidbit, this is the position
which will give you your best handgun accuracy for the shot.

These positions under discussion are the more important
basic ones. They have infinite modification in field shooting
with a handgun. There will be times when you Indian up on a

Standing but using tree for steadiness. This is deadly for short range handgun shooting. Note that both hands support the gun which is not allowed
to touch the tree. This position yields head shot accuracy at ruffed grouse,
but check your state game laws before doing this.

ground squirrel or woodchuck, when a down tree, a rock or stone fence will give you an opportunity to rest your gunhand across it for a steady, accucate shot. There will be times, occasionally, when you will have an opportunity for a prone shot —all these in addition to the conventional off-hand position, making your handgun shooting much more accurate and versatile.

The standing, off-hand position has merit for field shooting, don't ever forget that. But like the off-hand position with a rifle, skill in using it comes only after you have acquired proficiency in the other positions. Most riflemen start by using the prone position—a very wise choice—if they eventually get around to more practical field shooting positions, such as the sitting and standing. It is seldom, however, that one become a crack shot by immediately concentrating on the standing position, the most unstable of the lot.

That is also true of handgun shooting. Starting with the more stable positions, such as sitting and kneeling, a handgunner develops a *feel* for his revolver or pistol. He develops confidence in it and his own ability to do accurate field shooting because he immediately gets better than fair results —something which is seldom possible when he starts directly in the off-hand shooting position.

The secret of accurate handgun shooting, as in rifles, is trigger control. It is especially important in handgun shooting because your firearm is much more unstable than a rifle. Once your ability to squeeze off a shot carefully, while keeping your sights aligned, becomes habit, all the rest of handgun shooting techniques are easily mastered. Preliminary practice of the trigger squeeze is best done from the more stable positions, for then the entire technique of shooting can be carefully broken down into its several component parts: steady holding, proper sight and range picture, and trigger squeeze.

Uniform pressure must be put on the trigger, increasing it until the handgun is fired. You must, at the same time, *see* your target right. You must keep those sights *on* during the entire process.

You will notice that your sights are never at rest, regardless of your shooting position. There is always some movement. The degree of this movement is conditioned by the position you use. In off-hand shooting you will find your sights describing a circle on your target. The size of this circle will depend on your ability to hold steadily, and it will become consistently smaller with practice. If your trigger squeeze is right, and you have no tendency to jerk, your shot will always hit within the circle on your target described by your sights.

This backwoods technique of using a handgun is a long way down the ridge from the romantic concept of handling revolvers, but it get results. There will be greater accuracy in field shooting with a handgun, and indirectly it will make you a better rifle shot.

A revolver or pistol emphasizes trajectories, the importance of steady holding, trigger control. After mastering practical handgun shooting on such game as squirrel, rabbit or woodchuck, a rifle feels exceptionally stable in your hands. Its long sighting radius, its weight, its flat trajectory all make it seem a relatively simple matter. When that big whitetail buck comes crashing out of a laurel thicket in a shower of snow, you know him for the easy target he is: big, and comparatively easy to hit. You stand there complete master of the situation because you have hit smaller, more difficult targets with a handgun at those short woods ranges.

It takes a sharp eye sometimes to see him. Sure he's smart, too. He'll sharpen up your hunting skills for that dream buck usually found in the same type cover.

PART V

Shotguns: Equipment, Care and Cleaning

CHAPTER 12

Shotguns For Small Game Shooting

It has been said that rifle shooting is a science, shotgun shooting an art.

A hunter can have no quarrel with that, I suppose. But like all generalizations it is subject to qualification. All great game shots are more artist than scientist. They all have the subjective viewpoint of the artist, both in the selection of firearms, and in their use. I have never known any outstanding field shots who didn't have individual peculiarities of shooting and stalking which affected their choice of calibers and gauges. This, in large measure, accounts for the diversity of opinion on proper field guns.

What is the best shotgun for ruffed grouse, squirrel and rabbit shooting—the best degree of choke and shot size? Ever toss that question into an evening discussion around an autumn camp? It is surprising the difference of opinion, and it is surprising the number of hunters behind those opinions who make them pay off, autumn after autumn on upland birds and small game.

They use different tools, as it were, but basically the skills they bring to field shooting are the same. Usually they are good all around field shots, both with shotguns and rifles. Their upland shooting with shotguns is only a segment of their whole pattern of field shooting. They are equally at home with a rifle in their hands, hunting the heavy cover when deer season rolls around.

Such general, over-all shooting modifies shotgun use

somewhat. It also loosens up a hunter's rifle shooting technique. It modifies shotgun selection, too, but not as much as would appear at first glance. Obviously there is no logic in going to a bolt action shotgun because you use a bolt action rifle for deer. It is good practice, however, to use a pump action shotgun, if you are using a slide action rifle. Modification, though, should be more in stocking, trigger pull, weight to some extent, and recoil. In short, those modifications should be such, that in going from your deer and small game rifles to a shotgun for squirrel, rabbit or ruffed grouse, you get that, "I believe we have met before," feeling when you snap your shotgun to your shoulder.

Subconscious shooting habits take over in game shooting. When a ruffed grouse explodes out of a hazel thicket in front of your hard working springer, twisting and turning through the multi-colored cover, you are not going to consciously lead it, consciously cheek your gun in a certain way. All those details, win, lose or draw, have already been decided. Some by the stocking of your shotgun, some by the amount of ruffed grouse you have shot, more by the type of hunter you are—your personality. You make the shot, or you miss. And that also goes into the sum total of your experience, a contribution which will be totaled on your next try.

With this in mind, let's consider the more tangible assets of shotguns and loads for small game and bird shooting. First, though, let's examine some of the factors which bring rifle and shotgun shooting closer together.

A good shotgun for small game shooting must be fast handling. It must have just sufficient weight to swing steadily and absorb recoil. This adds up to a gun weighing from 6 to 7½ pounds. These qualifications also add up to a very nice deer rifle for snapshooting, with the exception of the one item of weight. Deer rifles of fairly heavy recoil could use a bit more weight than this.

Shotgun fit means that the pattern is nicely centered on your target when you snap your gun to your shoulder. *Essential fit, with either rifle or shotgun, means that a hunter should find it extremely awkward to avoid looking down the sights when the piece is mounted.*

His trigger hand should seem awkward in any place except at the grip of the stock, the forefinger on the trigger. Anything less than this, with either rifle or shotgun, means that the hunter is adapting himself to the gun, rather than the gun being adapted to him.

Just recently I had a custom stocking job done on a Model 71, .348 Winchester. The finished job weighed 8½ pounds. But with the nicely fitted stock and the superb balance of the rifle, it seems at least a pound lighter.

My big game shooting with this rifle is very similar to that of upland shotgunners taking ruffed grouse, except that my game with this rifle requires that I often make a precision shot on squirrel, as well as fast moving snapshots at deer and elk.

Let's examine the stocking of this rifle to see if there is any essential difference between such rifles and a shotgun stocked for upland bird shooting. Length of pull 13¼ inches, drop at comb 1⅝, drop at heel 2¼, drop at heel of the Monte Carlo 1¾ and downward pitch 3¼ inches. In comparison, my Remington 20 gauge pump has the following stock dimensions; length to pull 13⅞ inches, drop at comb 1¾, drop at heel 2½ and pitch 1½.

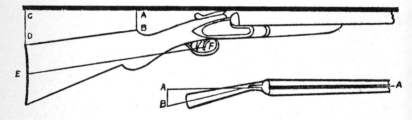

Dimensions of a stock: (*Top*) A-B, drop at comb; C-D, drop at heel; E-F, length of stock. (*Bottom*) A, center line of barrel or rib; A-B, cast-off.

The only essential difference between these stockings is in the stock length and downward pitch. The shorter stock of the rifle is made necessary by the fact that when the deer season rolls around it is colder, and one wears more clothing. A gun designed for snapshooting under the circumstances must have a shorter stock to handle properly. The difference in pitch is accounted for by the nature of the targets. Ruffed grouse always rise to the shot. A pitch of more than 1½ inches gives a

Remington pump shotgun—in 20 gauge, one of my favorites.

shotgun a tendency to shoot low, nicking the game with the ragged edge of the pattern because the two factors of gun mounting and flushing birds are at cross purposes.

One favored ruffed grouse cover of mine is a series of warm south-lying slopes. I work this time after time during the autumn shooting. The ruffed grouse spiral up through the trees to gain elevation, then plane across the brush to drop into the cover again. Here is tricky snapshooting. I must make a play for one of those comparatively open spots in the alders, get on my game as it rockets through, making the shot the instant the butt of my gun touches my shoulder. There are two leads with which to contend, forward and upward. The forward lead is made as my gun comes to my shoulder. The thunderous upward spiraling of my flushed grouse is taken care of by having just enough pitch in the stocking to throw patterns a trifle high.

Later in the season, when I am catfooting along these same alder slopes with my .348 Winchester, deer on my mind, the targets are essentially the same. Of course there is no necessity for any stock compensation to make my rifle shoot high. Those old gray faced bucks are not going out through the tops of the alder when I jump them, though it would seem as if they were when a big old buster comes crashing out of his bed. A downward pitch of 3 inches places my front sight on exactly the spot I want to hit, when my rifle is snapped to my shoulder.

With the exception of these two deviations, my rifle and shotgun are essentially the same. Is there any difference in handling them? Do you sight a rifle and point a shotgun, as is often explained by any number of clever writers on the subject? Thirty years of hunting makes me very doubtful. Of course it depends on what these experts mean by sighting. I think you point it, more or less.

If a hunter spends any appreciable length of time "drawing a bead," and "centering the crosshairs" on his target rifle shooting, one thing is indicated. He simply has a rifle which doesn't fit him properly.

As rifle and shotgun stocking is brought closer together, snapshooting techniques are very closely wedded. That rifle bullet, after all, merely represents the *exact* center of your killing pattern. Of course, you glance through your rifle sights as your gun touches your shoulder—proper stocking takes care of that. For long field shots you are more precise in your alignment. You may even use one of the more stable shooting positions to give you a bit more accuracy. But within the range limits of heavy cover, snapshooting with a rifle or shotgun, the shooting techniques tend to merge. If that merger is encouraged by careful stocking, it is surprising how much of your ruffed grouse shooting skills rub off on your big game shooting, once you are committed to the autumn deer coverts, a big buck in mind.

Best barrel lengths for upland shotgun are 26 to 28 inches, depending on the action. A pump or auto loading shotgun, with their longer receivers, are best with 26 inch barrels. A double, or over and under should carry 28 inch tubes for most effective handling. It depends a lot on balance. I have seen trim 20 gauge doubles with 30 inch barrels which handled fast, and pointed out extremely well because they were properly stocked. I have also handled other shotguns with much shorter barrels, which were so totally lacking in balance, nothing short of a complete rebuilding could have corrected the faults.

The heart of an upland shotgun is in the choke. Other factors of shotgun shooting may be compromised and a fair amount of hits still obtained. But the choke must be right for the average range, the touch and go of ruffed grouse, rabbit and squirrel shooting, or all the other gilt edge qualifications, such as proper balance, barrel length, weight and trigger pull, are ineffective.

All upland gunning is short range, with most of the shooting within 25-35 yards. At this range, even the improved cylinder choke is throwing full choke patterns. Where the range is extended to 35 yards, as may occur when shooting cottontail

One of Browning's long popular Superposed line of Over/Under shotguns.

rabbits in front of hounds, a modified choke delivering 60 percent at 40 yards is on target with a 70 percent pattern.

Your two best chokes, especially in combination, are modified and improved cylinder for short range shooting. These, in a light 20 gauge double, using 1 ounce shot charges, will cover all ranges out to a full 40 yards. Where the gun is a single-barrel, the best selection is improved cylinder or, better yet, a pump or automatic with an adjustable choke.

I cannot see any place in upland gunning for more open Skeet choke, unless it is backed by a modified choke. But there is a definite place for spreader, or brush loads that give more open patterns for extremely short range 20-25 yard shooting. These spreader or brush loads are manufactured in 12 gauge by several of the larger ammunition suppliers such as Winchester-Western and Remington-Peters.

Best ruffed grouse shotgun I ever owned was a Richland 20 gauge double with 26 inch barrels. This gun, bored modified and improved cylinder, delivered excellent 60 and 45 percent patterns at 40 yards. It also delivered excellent uniform patterns with spreader loads, either factory make or handloads of my own contriving. This gun was an excellent compromise of proper weight, gauge and barrel length. Tipping the scales at 6 pounds, it was no burden at the end of a full day's hunt.

Present-day shotguns in the three more popular gauges, 20, 16 and 12, handle about the same shot charge weights, and with about the same patterning efficiency. While the 16 gauge is becoming more or less obsolete, with the 20 and 12 gauge about equally popular, the shot charge weights remain about the same over the years, $\frac{7}{8}$, 1, $1\frac{1}{16}$, $1\frac{1}{8}$, $1\frac{3}{16}$, and $1\frac{1}{4}$ ounces.

For upland shooting the three or four first named weights are the more popular. There is no ballistic reason for more than 1⅛ ounces of shot with any shot size where the ranges are this side of 35 yards. There are several very good reasons for using an even lighter shot charge. Where the emphasis is on light guns for upland shooting, light shot charge weights are definitely indicated. Recoil is always a factor in all gunning. A fast, dynamic gun with no apparent recoil is a must for all upland gunning, regardless of the gauge selected.

Present-day 28 gauge shotguns handle about the same shot charge weights as those associated with the 20 gauge only a few years ago. During the past decade, with the use of ⅞ and 1 ounce shot charges, the 28 gauge has come into its own as an upland gauge. It is especially attractive in a double, side by side, or as a neat over-under.

How about the most effective shot sizes for upland game? Most hunters consider shot sizes from 6 to 7½ just the ticket for ruffed grouse. My own preference is for the smaller sized 7½ for this type shooting. Quail shooters usually prefer 7½ to 8's, while squirrel and rabbit hunters are partial to size 6. Size 7½ shot in 20 gauge has worked well for me on rabbit, especially jump shooting bunnies without the aid of dogs. And for that matter, a close shooting 20 gauge throwing an ounce of size 6 shot makes a very effective load for both squirrel and rabbit.

One qualification to any arbitrary selection for shot size for specific game lies in the peculiarities of shotguns themselves. Some guns will handle only one or two shot sizes well. Others may have a versatility which enables a hunter to use several shot sizes and get good dense, uniform killing patterns. If your shotgun patterns best with 7½ size shot, and your quarry is rabbit, stick to that close shooting pattern, even though you consider them a bit small for your game. A ragged pattern of 6's doesn't have the killing potential of an even, dense pattern of 7½ shot, all paper ballistics to the contrary.

Of course, if you are using a single barrel pump or autoloading shotgun, the addition of one of several choking devices presently available will give a greater selectivity of pattern. You may discover just the right degree of choke to handle those heavier shot sizes, when they are called for.

But even with a choke device, such as the splendid Poly Choke, you must still match the obtainable pattern with the degree of choke. You cannot arbitrarily say you want 70 percent patterns at 25 yards with some special shot size, set your

A popular shotgun today, the Remington Model 1100 semiautomatic. This one is their Skeet gun. It can be gotten in a 20 ga. lightweight version.

choking device for modified pattern, and know you are getting the desired results. You may be getting only 45 percent patterns or better than 70 percent. It is only after long sessions at a pattern board that you really know, in terms of field effectiveness, the degree of choke setting which gives you what you want with some certain shot size.

Shotgun preferences for upland gunning are more subjective than deer rifle preferences, if that is possible.

When anyone arbitrarily tells you this is your best gun for ruffed grouse, without qualification, question his field experience. The more time an autumn gunner spends in upland cover, the more mellow he becomes. He knows there are too many right answers to proper shotgun selection for him to be arbitrary about it.

There is nothing more beautiful than a well made double gun. There is nothing more practical and efficient in ruffed grouse cover, or for tumbling a bunny in front of a frantic beagle, knocking a squirrel out of a beechnut. But, cannot the same things be said about our better grade pump action shotguns, an over and under, an autoloading shotgun?

The whole problem of shotgun selection, even use, simmers down to personal preferences. I have merely traced a few of the pathways you will travel toward that ultimate shotgun which you will eventually own, and swear by—after several autumns of upland gunning.

CHAPTER 13

The Makings Of A Small Game Hunter

Out West they call it the "makings." If you have tobacco and cigarette papers you have the "makings" of a smoke. If you have killed a brace of blue grouse, you have the "makings" of a stew. The "makings" of a small game hunter are those essential bits of equipment which make a definite contribution to the success of a hunt.

Take the item of proper clothing for example. How many small game hunters actually wear clothing which makes a direct contribution to the overall success of their day afield? Not many.

Most small game is alarmed by about the same things as the big game, which you will eventually hunt. When you go prepared for the one type of hunting, then you are prepared for the other, so far as proper clothing is concerned, except for color. In addition to being alarmed by the same type of *unusual* noise as big game, the smaller game are touched off by other factors which deer and elk do not find alarming. Both deer and elk find it difficult to distinguish a hunter at rest. But ruffed grouse, and squirrel will both distinguish silhouette and color.

You will not get much squirrel or grouse shooting dressed in scarlet, though a touch of red is essential for protection from other hunters. Best bet is a red hunting hat or cap, with the rest of your clothing neutral to blend in with the browns and golds of the multi-colored autumn woods.

Clothing for grouse and squirrel shooting, or rabbit hunting should be as soft as a fawn's coat. It should only whisper, or remain silent when it touches the cover. Let the other hunters have their harsh canvas hunting coats and trousers, with their propensity to scrape against each bush or bough with harsh, unusual noise, totally foreign to the cover, and double alarming for that reason. It is better that you go dressed in light wool, or woolen and cotton outer garments, even at the expense of getting damp occasionally.

For those real old stinkers of a day there is nothing better than light nylon rain clothes. These should be large enough to slip over your regular hunting clothes, and can be removed when the weather clears. They are not bulky, and can be carried, during questionable weather, in the back of your hunting jacket.

Remember what I said about a great hunting dog reflecting his master's ability afield, and that back of each great dog there was also a great hunter? The same factors enter into a hunter's field dress. Just as surely as you find a good all around hunter, you also find a man who is very careful in his selection of clothing, equipment and guns. Nothing is left to chance. Anything which will contribute to the success of the hunt is carefully considered.

Shoes have ruined more hunting trips than any lack of game. What are good field shoes? Here is my selection after a quarter of a century of hunting. For deer, grouse, or other game, good field shoes should be made of leather with tops 10 inches high, crepe rubber soles thick enough that you do not feel each rock or stick on which you step. There is only one quality leather—the best.

Shoes of this type will serve for bird hunting. They are excellent in the squirrel woods, and for stillhunting deer, they are a must. The crepe rubber soles give you quiet going. They cushion your step for tireless, all day tramping.

Please note those 10 inch top requirements. They are very much more important than would at first appear. A top higher than this tends to bind the muscles of the legs. Hunting shoes with 16 and 18 inch tops are especially at fault in this. In addition to binding the legs, those higher tops add needlessly to the weight of field shoes, making them very tiring to wear for a day's hunt. A 10 inch top comes below the calf of the leg, but is sufficiently high to give comfortable support to the feet in walking.

Shoe fit is most important, yet few outdoorsmen really

know what is meant by the word. A shoe properly fitted, should not make you conscious of your feet, uphill or down, all day long. To achieve such fit requires plenty of test and try, plenty of testing the various lasts: narrow, medium, wide. Plenty of trying various brands until you get a shoe which feels right to your feet.

You must remember that in hiking and hunting, there is a tendency for the feet to swell slightly. A shoe which is just right for normal street wear is seldom the correct size for field use. It may feel comfortable enough in the morning, but after a day's tramp in the woods with your dog, hunting ruffed grouse, that snugness grows to a painful tightness.

A good rule is to buy your hunting shoes about one size larger than street shoes, then fill them with extra pairs of socks. Best bet for such sock is a light inner woolen one, with a medium weight woolen outer sock. By wearing two pair of socks with your outdoor shoes you have much better insulation than you would have with one heavy pair of woolen socks. And, of course, if your feet do have a tendency to swell, one pair may be removed afield to correct the fit.

Hunting shoes should be bought and properly broken in several weeks before your planned hunting trips. In breaking in field shoes work plenty of neatsfoot oil into the leather, both from the inside and outside of your shoes. This will make them soft and pliable. After this soft leather has set to your feet, from making several short hiking trips, and from wear around the house, treat your shoes with any one of several brands of leather dressing and water proofing compounds presently on the market.

There is only one good material for shoe laces, leather. They should be well oiled before use. One other item should be used with these laces, too. For a comfortable fit, as well as to keep your shoe laces from eventually wearing through the tongue of your hunting shoes, have your shoe repair man make you two false tongues for your hunting shoes.

These are two pieces of soft leather about two inches wide and eight inches in length. You may cut them an inch or so longer than this to allow for a leather fringe at the bottom, logger fashion, making for a bit more dressy appearing outdoor shoe. Two holes are punched at the bottom of your false tongues through which the lacings are passed before placing them in your hunting shoes. These false tongues are very valuable additions to any hunting shoe, and once you have used them you will recognize their merits at once.

Hunting shoes, of the type I have described here, are exemplified by Chippewa, Bass, Red Wing, and Russell. Any of these brands have very high quality oil tanned leather in their makeup. There are several other, less expensive hunting shoes on the market which appear to be bargains, but in the long run, are more expensive and much less serviceable than those high quality brand name shoes. After a few trips afield with those cheap hunting shoes, one realizes that they lose their shape, and are impossible fits. The leather from which they are made is usually split cowhide, so porous they will not turn dampness, even with the best waterproof leather dressing.

When it is wet and you are hunting late autumn squirrel, rabbit or ruffed grouse, there is nothing to equal rubber for footwear. Like your leather hunting shoes, your rubber ones should be a size larger than footwear for street use. They also should be worn with two pair of medium weight woolen socks to afford proper insulation. The requirements of a good rubber hunting shoe are about the same as those of leather: 10 inch top and just the proper fit without binding. The only excuse for rubber shoes or packs with higher than 10 inch tops is deep snow or wet ground where a 16 inch top affords more protection.

These rubber packs may be obtained with lacings extending to the instep, or they may be had with ankle fit legs, and lacings at the top. I personally prefer the latter. Properly fitted they are less binding around the leg, but are still snug enough for all day hiking without chafing.

The Maine hunting boot, a somewhat glorified name for a plain pair of rubbers (essentially) with sewed-on leather uppers. But they are very popular and have their advantages, particularly when the going is wet. They minimize foot perspiration.

There is one other type of shoe available which has merit for many types of small game hunting. This is the rubber footed, leather topped shoe pack, quite often used when hunting in snow—small game or large. These are very good, if the tops are made of the best quality leather which can be treated to waterproof them. But if they are made of inferior leather, melting snow will seep into your packs regardless of your waterproofing.

A handwarmer is one piece of small game hunting "makings" which makes a direct contribution to good shooting. They are light to carry, but have a ton of comfort in them on a cold autumn morning when you are prowling a ruffed grouse cover or hunting rabbits. Keep one in your pocket and warm your trigger hand occasionally.

Binoculars, of course, are essential for any type of hunting or hiking. In my book, *Art of Successful Deer Hunting* a chapter is devoted to their selection and use. It is sufficient here to point out their importance in small game hunting. Select the best, learn to use them, and you will be surprised at the new world they open for you.

Learning to use them is something very few hunters actually do. They adjust them to their eyes for all distances from about a hundred feet to infinity, and let it go at that. In doing this they are not realizing the full potential of their binoculars, for there is another adjustment on your binoculars with which you should experiment—the close in focusing which gives you a stereoscopic effect from about twenty-five to one hundred and fifty feet. In heavy cover, with your binoculars set for this close viewing, you can see through thickets, down the small avenues of the forest, and examine an oak or beechnut harboring squirrel. It is a revelation to hunters who have only used their binoculars for longer viewing.

The small game and varmint sniper has another piece of equipment which the average squirrel or rabbit hunter would find awkward and impractical. That is a good spotting scope. It is surprising the lost opportunities a hunter has on a day's woodchuck or ground squirrel shooting, unless he has some means of searching the cover in detail out there at two and three hundred yards. Piles of fresh dirt along an old stone fence are evidence of woodchuck workings in clover fields and along creek banks. These will be spotted with binoculars, but for more detailed study of game activity at such distances,

The Bushnell Banner (7X-12X) Zoom Binocular.

there is nothing which will take the place of a good spotting scope.

In selecting one for your field use, remember that the stand is almost as important as the scope itself. The stand should be low in silhouette, because you will usually use it from the prone position. It should be sturdy and wide angled to give a stable support to the spotting scope. Unless it meets all these requirements, the high power of your spotting scope is lost.

Best power in a spotting scope for general use ranges from 15 to 25X. I personally prefer the 25X scope. A spotting scope should take over where binoculars leave off. There is no use in carrying a scope of 10X power when you are using 7 X 35 binoculars. A 25X spotting scope takes over where medium powered binoculars leave off.

The Sentry model Bushnell spotting scope with shooter's stand.

A spotting scope is not only a fine way of currying your hunting cover in detail, studying game and game habitat, but it is also excellent for spotting those unaccountable misses at the longer ranges. Where is my rifle shooting under actual field conditions, at estimated ranges? That can only be answered by your hunting partner spotting your shots while you try your skill at a few typical field shots.

Last season, while hunting ground squirrel, I got three straight misses at ranges around two hundred yards, my first three shots of the day. In the tall sear grass of late August, shots were difficult to spot through my hunting scope. There would be an obscuring puff of dust around my target, and that was all. Was it high, low, right or left?

Out of my rucksack came the spotting scope. The next target, a big old grizzled ground squirrel of aldermanic proportions, was carefully focused in the 25X field of my Bushnell spotting scope by my partner. At the shot he said just one word, "High." I clicked my elevation down a point. Another shot some fifteen minutes later, with the spotting scope again set up and focused on my target, was a different story. This time my partner said, "On, but still a bit high for the range." Another quarter point of elevation correction and I was all set for the day.

A spotting scope afield poses the problem of transportation. They are bulky and cumbersome to carry, and you are not constantly using them, either. During a day's hunt after ground squirrel or woodchuck, there are plenty of short range opportunities where ordinary binoculars give you sufficient power for detailed observation. Best method of carrying a spotting scope is in a rucksack. Fact is, a rucksack is almost a must for any outdoor activity from hiking to big game hunting. I use one constantly on my small game excursions to not only carry my spotting scope, but also for such items as camera, light meter, extra ammunition, lunch, and all the odds and ends of equipment which I might use during the day.

Selecting a rucksack for small game hunting requires plenty of thought and plenty of testing. There are several bulky canvas bags designed for cargo carrying, such as bedding, tents and equipment on a portage, but which are not practical for small game hunting. A rucksack for hunting should be on the small side. It should have plenty of wide pockets for storing items of equipment. Another requirement is that it ride high between your shoulders where it will not touch the cover as you move about. Shoulder straps should be wide, but not bulky or padded, unless such padding can be slipped down the shoulder strap on the shoulder you normally shoot from. Any padding here is very apt to throw your carefully stocked rifle out of balance.

For my own use this adds up to a light tubular frame pack-

The popular Sportsman compass distributed by Michael's of Oregon. Slips easily in a pocket, is thin and is lightweight insurance for checking directions. Good idea also to carry along a map portion covering unfamiliar terrain, as when hunting new areas.

sack. It has plenty of room for an overnight camping outfit, when I am off on a back country hiking and hunting trip.

There are several other rucksacks available which serve the purposes of a small game hunter quite well. A small Duluth-type pack is excellent. So is the Norwegian type rucksack with its many outside pockets.

You will be surprised at the many items of equipment which eventually find their way into your rucksack such as an extra jacket to slip on during the early morning hours when an autumn nip to the air makes for cold hunting. There will also be times when Indian summer touches the cover like a benediction and you will appreciate a rucksack for carrying your hunting coat and gloves.

All in all, the "makings" of a small game hunter means the difference between going prepared for an enjoyable day

The rucksack for hunting should hang well between the shoulders so as not to catch on brush. It should be large enough to contain a small handaxe, Nylon shelter-half, and emergency rations for a couple of days, including a good supply of matches in a waterproof container. The rucksack's contents will vary with the type of country hunted, but details should be worked out during your small game hunting—the training ground for big game hunting.

afield, with equipment which enables you to take every advantage of your hunting, and being less prepared for eventualities. Field experience will tend to make such equipment highly individual, just as field experience will make its selection highly practical. When your "makings" are right, your hunt is off to a good start.

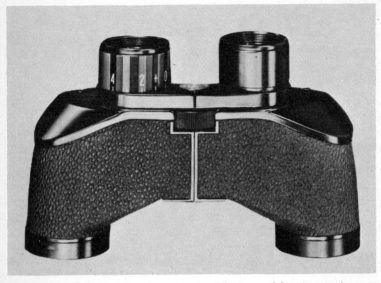

A good pair of binoculars is a very useful piece of hunting equipment. This one is another Bushnell model.

CHAPTER 14

Care And Cleaning Of Guns And Equipment

Good firearms deserve good care. That would seem obvious, but it is surprising how many rifles and shotguns are not at top field shooting proficiency because they have been abused or neglected. Much of this neglect stems from the fact that many hunters believe that with the inception of non-mercuric, non-corrosive primers there is little reason for cleaning firearms. But that isn't so. Non-mercuric, non-corrosive primers have simplified cleaning, but they have not eliminated it.

I put in a day in ruffed grouse cover recently, hunting from good daylight until a severe storm canceled out my day. During the forenoon a brilliant sun played hide and seek with the racing stormclouds. My shotgun was exposed to a muggy heat which moistened the barrels with sweat from my hands. In midafternoon the thunder caps piling up against the hills touched off a rainstorm which lasted the better part of two hours.

After the hunt I had the not unpleasant chore of cleaning my shotgun before putting it back into the rack. First I took the barrels down. Examination of the tubes showed drops of water inside near the muzzle—something which would pit those mirror smooth barrels within twenty-four hours, unless the shotgun was properly cleaned and oiled before being put away.

Several dry flannel patches passed through the barrels with my cleaning rod served to mop up the moisture and removed all powder residue. But to make doubly sure, I changed my last patch and warmed it thoroughly in front of the fireplace before the final swabbing.

The outside of the barrels and all metal work received this same dry treatment with a flannel rag. Then I passed a brass brush through both tubes to loosen and remove any lead which might have collected from my field shooting. The heart of a shotgun lies in those mirror smooth tubes, and a brass brush is the best method of keeping them polished to perfection. This insures a minimum of shot deformation—good uniform patterns.

Any pitting, any minute roughness in a shotgun barrel is paid for by spotty patterns. You cannot be too careful in this final polishing and cleaning. Send your brass brush back and forth several times. Don't be afraid of injuring the choke. Brass brushes are comparatively soft; shotgun barrels are made of good modern steel.

After polishing with a brass brush, I swabbed the bore with some Gunslick bore cleaner designed to neutralize any residue from the powder or primer mixture. There are several other excellent preparations for this purpose on the market. Hoppe's No. 9 is good. So is Palma Compound.

A light gun grease should be used on the outside metal parts of your gun as a protection. This should be applied immediately after the arm has been dried. It should also be reapplied before field use. A bit of grease worked into the in-letting where wood and steel is joined, before going afield, serves to protect the wood from moisture, preventing swelling and warping under normal use.

Forearms and stocks should be gone over carefully with a dry rag, removing all moisture, sweat and oil residue after a day afield. Once the stock is thoroughly dry, examine the finish. That beautiful myrtlewood stock, or black figured walnut, will be beautiful only so long as it is taken care of, both in the field and after the hunting trip.

Probably more misinformation has been put out about stock finish than any one thing connected with guns.

The late Alvin Linden recommended a good grade of spar varnish, applied in several thin coats, to obtain that so-called "Linden oil finish." And Old Scratch, as Linden was called by outdoorsmen, probably knew more about stocks and stock finishes than any one man in the profession. Experiments have shown that wood treated with boiled linseed oil, beloved of many gunners for an oil finish, will absorb water just about as readily as untreated wood.

There are several oil type finishes on the market, however, which are excellent for protecting and enhancing the beauty of a striking piece of stock wood. A good oil type finish is marketed under the name of Lin-Speed. While these finishes have some linseed oil in their makeup, they have additional properties which seal the wood with a moisture-proof seal.

A stock of beautiful wood is a joy forever. But in field use it will eventually become marred. Scratches will appear in spite of your best field care. These can be removed with steel wool when they become too conspicuous, and the stock refinished without trouble.

One of my gunstocks, a beautiful light colored myrtle wood, made for me at Art Richardson's Gun Shop, Coquille, Oregon, has had two seasons in the squirrel and deer woods. This stock is now more beautiful than the day it was placed on the rifle. Occasional scratches are carefully worked out of the wood. After a trip afield, I dry it carefully, then touch it up with a bit of Lin-Speed Stock Finish, working the finish into the wood with the tips of my fingers.

Two seasons of use have materially darkened the fiddleback myrtle from which this stock is made. It now has the color appearance of a well used old violin.

Rifle and handgun cleaning pose about the same problems as that of shotgun care. Barrels should be well oiled and free from moisture when they are laid aside for any appreciable length of time. Pass a few dry patches through the bore immediately after field use. Then swab with patches moistened with Hoppe's number 9, or some other good bore cleaner. The bore should be wiped out before field use, or you may up the pressure of your first shot needlessly.

There is one other precaution in the care of rifles which should be watched. During the cold, blustery days of autumn when the storms are on the make, moisture sometimes collects in rifle barrels from flakes of snow. These often congeal into ice. A rifle, such as a .30/06, a .243 Winchester, etc. or other high intensity weapons, can very easily bulge the barrel, or even wreck the gun, when fired with such an obstruction in the tube.

After a hunting season is a memory, and you are storing your guns for the year, especial precautions should be taken to see that they come through this inactive period in good condition. Obviously, they should be stored in a dry, well ventilated place. Those requirements are usually met in any

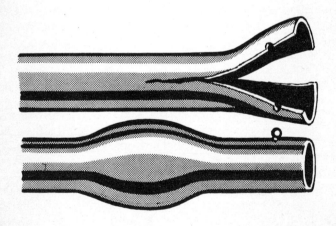

Whether it's ice, dirt or what have you, always watch out for barrel obstructions. The illustration shows what can happen when a shotgun having an obstructed barrel is fired.

well warmed house. Where most riflemen fall down in storing firearms is in the final preparations in cleaning and oiling. A fairly heavy gun grease, applied liberally inside and out after the final cleaning, will protect your firearms for months. The application of this grease to the bore should come only *after* two of three final cleanings and inspections have shown that there is not the least vestige of rust or powder fouling in the gun.

Do not plug the barrel with a rag under the mistaken idea that you are keeping moisture out. Leave it open. Allow the air to carry off any moisture due to the sweating of the steel.

Sling straps should be carefully oiled before being taken afield. Best for this is neatsfoot oil, well worked into the leather. Apply as much as the leather will absorb, returning to this task several times before going afield. This will keep it soft and pliable, even when it is subject to wet weather.

In selecting sling straps, incidentally, be sure you are getting the best of leather, or all your oiling and care will not help. Avoid those spongy leather straps. Select those made from the best oil tanned calf hide. Best of the carrying straps which I have used are those "Guide Straps" put out by Williams Gunsight Co., Davison, Michigan. These in the best grade come in hand tooled leather. They are light, and complement a beautiful gun in every particular.

Another firm with an outstandingly fine line of swivels, slings, straps and accessories is Michaels of Oregon. Write them at P.O. Box 13010, Portland, Oregon 97213 for a free catalog of their line which includes quick-detachable as well as standard slings and mounts.

Revolver and pistol holsters should receive applications of neatsfoot oil. Work the oil into your holsters until they are thoroughly saturated, both inside and out. Wipe off the surface oil so that it will not get on your hunting clothes. Now you have a holster which will give maximum protection to your sidearm at all times.

There is no justifiable reason for neglecting firearms on hunting trips. Just a little thought given to the problem of field cleaning materials will turn up a light, compact field cleaning kit. A jointed cleaning rod which can be taken down for transportation, a small can of bore cleaner, a tube of gun grease, a few dozen flannel patches, and you are all prepared for any field eventuality, such as storms and severe weather.

Your gun should be gone over nightly around the camp-fire, then stored for the night in a dry place, not too close to the fire, lest you fog your scope, or dry unevenly the wood of your carefully stocked rifle, causing it to change its center of impact.

All in all, the care and cleaning of small game guns and equipment is not an unpleasant task. There are a lot of fine hunting memories wrapped up in the chore, and it is the one way to insure the superb accuracy built into your guns.

PART VI

The Game

CHAPTER 15

Rabbit Hunting

The cottontail rabbit is our most universal game. There isn't a state in the Union in which he isn't hunted. Farm boy with his single barrel mail order shotgun, sportsman with his imported, expensive double, they all go for cottontail rabbit hunting. He is an excellent target for riflemen stillhunting with a .22 rifle. The number of rabbits killed each season reaches astronomical proportions.

Some are taken rabbit hunting; many are taken when outdoorsmen are hunting other game. One very good hunter of my acquaintance, while he will not shoot rabbit when hunting deer, always considers it a good omen when he jumps a few cottontails. If they are found out in the open at this time, very likely deer also will be outside the heavier cover. Like deer they have a propensity for feeding early mornings and late evenings. Again, like deer, they have the happy faculty of spending the day where they can soak up the late season warmth.

To find good rabbit hunting, like deer hunting, you must relate your game to the best available forage and cover conditions. This was indirectly touched upon in Chapter 2, Basic Hunting. It is re-emphasized here because of its importance. Obviously, no game stays in inhospitable cover by preference. The lush browse and the warm, storm sheltered range always prove more attractive.

If you find cover where frost lingers long after the sun has touched other sections with warmth, if you find cover which has scant browse, it is not good rabbit territory, nor good for any other game for that matter. The lush, overgrown, abandoned hill pastures, full of blackberry, short shrubs, clover, grass, wild cherry and sweet briar all indicate good hunting, for it adds up to warmth during the growing season and warmth during the late autumn when storms plaster the less sheltered sections with snow and sleet.

Cottontails are always plentiful in such cover. They are seldom found far from it unless pushed out by predators or heavy hunting. Good cover and game go together.

Ever hike through cottontail cover after the first fall of snow? Better yet, have you ever walked across snow sheltered fields during a full autumn moon when the light makes the entire cover a place of silver and shadow? If you have done this, you will be amused by the ludicrous antics, the downright enjoyment cottontail rabbits seem to get from this first fall of soft snow. They play, running in circles, leaping over bushes, chasing each other—dark shadows scurrying over the gleaming snow so fast your eyes can scarcely follow them.

Next morning the maze of tracks, apparently without rhyme or reason, testifies to the high revel they held during the night. Next morning, too, if you like to still hunt rabbit, developing skills which will make whitetail deer comparatively easy, you will find a very challenging quarry in these rabbits around the marge of those openings where they played during the full moon.

Cottontail   *Cottontail*
(Slow Hop)   *(Bounding)*

Cottontail tracks.

Work the edge of any hill, flat and high river bottom. Watch the cover for exit trails. Watch for sheltered places where any natural object cancels out winddrift, such as logs, stumps, rock ledges or slight rises in the ground. These are the places cottontails select for their forms. They snooze away the time between feeding periods or other activity in these sheltered spots.

Your best gun for this type of still hunting is a .22 rimfire rifle, using high speed hollow point bullets. This rifle should be a direct understudy of your big game rifle in action, stocking and sight.

Shots should be taken at the head, if your game is at rest. If you flush one and must take a running shot, then the aiming point should be the shoulder section, just the same as it will be on running deer.

The most essential gift a rabbit hunter can have is ability to see his quarry under almost impossible circumstances of cover and lighting. A cottontail blends in with about any background. And, until your eyes are trained to see properly, they are about the most inconspicuous game you ever hunted. Afterwards, when you have trained yourself, and acute observation is habitual, you will marvel how easily they are separated from their backgrounds. This ability to see will not only pay off in the small game field, but is also one of your most valuable assets in big game hunting.

Close observation is a matter of seeing in detail. It is more mind training than eye-sight. It has its foundation in keen curiosity, wanting to know what game and game sign have to tell you—from cottontail to moose. A skilled rabbit hunter, like all skilled hunters regardless of the game, is constantly evaluating cover, tracks and weather. He is relating these to the probable reaction of the game. He is reading a very interesting narrative of his game activity for the past twenty-four hours.

Stillhunting cottontails with a rifle is only one phase of this sport. When we include jackrabbit and snowshoe rabbit, the field for stillhunting is much expanded. Stillhunting jackrabbit has many of the elements of mule deer hunting in it. Stillhunting snowshoe rabbit requires plenty of good whitetail deer technique.

The snowshoe rabbit is more a creature of the big woods, the heavy cover sections, where you would normally hunt deer. Quite often he is found on the same range as whitetail deer. And in the mountains of the West he is found in the same cover as mule deer.

Fact is, while waiting for the annual migration of mule deer in the western foothills, I have spent plenty of time still-hunting snowshoe rabbit with my big game rifle, full powered loads, taking nothing but head shots. Usually, my best hunting would be along the jackpine thickets where bitterbrush and other low growing shrubs afforded plenty of lush feed and shelter. Late evening, at about the time you might expect deer to be on the move, or feeding, I would ease along the creek bottom, watching the open hillsides above me for snowshoe rabbit. This was early enough in the season that they still wore their brownish-grey coats, and were not as well camouflaged as they would be later in the snow when they were completely dressed in white. Invariably, within a short hunt from camp, I would get some shooting.

Later, when the mule deer were on the move, pouring out of their high summer ranges, the very places where I hunted snowshoe rabbit would be favored by those old grey faced bucks as stop-over points in their migrations. The reason for this being the favorable nature of the cover—food, concealing shelter, and warmth.

Stillhunting jackrabbit in the more open ranges has probably taught more western hunters how to hit running deer than any other type of game. Get a jack running across a sagebrush flat, his long ears layed back, darting in and out of the sagebrush, and if you nail him consistently with your rifle, all other shooting at moving targets will seem comparatively easy.

Another good point about this rangy member of the rabbit family is that there is no closed season on him. Want to put in a summer vacation brushing up on your shooting techniques? Just about any Western, or Midwestern ranch can accommodate you, especially if it is devoted to the raising of alfalfa hay or grain.

Best of rabbit hunting, however, is shooting cottontail or snowshoe rabbit in front of hounds. This phase of hunting is an art within itself.

Hunt a lifetime with hounds, your quarry rabbit, and still you will not come up with all the answers. The combination of rabbit and hound certainly doesn't lend itself to over simplification. Even the problem of what type hound to use for

Running jackrabbits pose challenging shots to the varmint shooter. When they stop running and sit up, they often pose some very, very long range shots.

this sport divides rabbit hunters into two distinct camps. There are those who want a fast hound, something which, as they contend, will make their quarry break cover. But, says your exponent of the slow hounds, your fast dog will ground a rabbit too quickly for best sport. Push a cottontail closely with a pack of fast dogs and it is away to his burrow without further ado.

A hunter cannot be neutral in this hound controversy and still be a dyed in the wool rabbit hunter. There is no middle ground. I am a slow hound man, myself, just as I am a slow hunter by nature, regardless of the type of game. A slow hound man has just two breeds of dogs in mind as suitable for rabbit hunting, Bassets and Beagles. Aside from the practical nature of this selection, there are aesthetic ones as well. Ever hear a Beagle belling across a wooded valley, the echoes full in the hemlocks? Ever hear a good chop mouthed Basset with a cottontail or snowshoe rabbit out front? Here is music to set your heart to dancing.

Here is something else, too. Just the right amount of speed to keep your quarry moving, without the compelling necessity of taking to earth.

When you put a trained Basset or Beagle down, watch the way he starts to work. In many ways this is the best part of your hunt. Those maze of rabbit tracks are eventually worked out; the exit trails from the openings are found. Then a tenative, mellow bay floats out of the thickets. Silence. Another mellow note, sincere and reassuring. Then he is in full cry, joined by his pack mate, if you are hunting two dogs.

If you have worked close with your dogs, watching the small lanes and openings to either side of the thickets, ten chances to one you are going to get an extra dividend of shooting. Cottontails will be flushed which your hounds are not trailing.

But this one they have jumped. Notice how straight away from his home cover he is running? Notice how he draws out the hounds? Intentional or otherwise, he is leading your dogs away from a fair concentration of his kind. But it is only for the moment.

Now is the time to plan your strategy. Move forward to the first opening the chase has crossed. Wait here. When that cottontail has unlimbered a bit he will circle. Those slow hounds, as persistent as tax collectors, are going to keep him on the move, and eventually the chase will end up on the home grounds. If you have selected a good position, and have the patience to wait it out, you will get a shot.

Snowshoe rabbits and cottontails have the same well defined trails as deer, and they are used for the same purpose. There are foraging trails through the lush browse; there are escape trails leading away from their forms, trails leading from one favored section of cover to another.

Their response to hunting is very similar to deer also, especially cottontail. Jump one in this section today, and tomorrow you have a fine chance for a repeat performance. Find a section well populated with cottontail or snowshoe rabbits this fall, and it is a fine place to return next autumn when the rabbit season opens.

Rabbits are the one game which will respond to the best

you can put into a hunt, running them with hounds or still hunting them with a .22 rifle. To be successful hunting rabbits you must use plenty of woodcraft, plenty of shooting skill. There should be just as much pride in bagging a mess of cottontail or snowshoe rabbits as there is in downing an elk, for both types of hunting levy equally on your ability as a woodsman and hunter. And while you hunt the former, you are getting wonderful training for hunting the latter.

CHAPTER 16

Raccoon Hunting

A raccoon's comings and goings, to an inexperienced hunter, are deeply clothed in mystery by his nocturnal habits. While occasionally he will be found abroad during overcast days, for the most part he starts his activities at dark. And what a range of activities they are!

Ever find fresh coon tracks along the marge of a swamp, and try to unravel the intricate wanderings? It is a most interesting and rewarding experience. For you will learn much about raccoon habit, and plenty about reading sign. Fact is, raccoons are your best teachers of sign reading. Become proficient in reading and interpreting the involved comings and goings of raccoons from their trail sign and all the rest is easy. Rabbit sign is an open book; that of deer is quite obvious. This masked bandit of the swamps and farmlands has had his wits sharpened by constant hunting over a period of two hundred years. He never does any of the expected things. And, while his curiosity sometimes betrays him, he never does any of the stupid things which are constantly tripping up lesser game.

Here, as the dark shadows lengthen across the swamp, and evening is still full of the vesper sounds of sleepy minded birds, his majesty, the American Raccoon descends from his den tree. He is out for a night of feeding, frolicking and fighting, a buccaneering that is the hall mark of raccoons.

During warm weather he is very apt to sleep out the day in the forks of a sun-warmed, moss covered swamp oak, maple or other tree which affords him plenty of privacy. Af-

Raccoon

terwards, as the season advances, he will take to a warm hollow tree, snuggling in with anywhere from two to a half dozen of his kind. If the weather turns extremely cold, he will go into semihibernation.

But this late summer evening, when he descends from his tree, he has no thought of hibernation in mind. He wants food and adventure. Listen quietly along the marge of the swamp, or in an orchard or cornfield, and often you will hear a squalling, rip-snorting fight. This will be two old swamp coon staging a knock-down and dragout battle over some choice tidbit they have uncovered. In my orchard, late of an autumn night, I have heard such fights time after time. Taking my flashlight and investigating, I may find two raccoons in a Baldwin apple tree. And even though the apple tree is loaded with fruit, there just isn't enough room for two strange raccoons to eat peacefully.

The only ones which seem to get along without fighting are those of a single clan, a family consisting of a sow coon and half grown young ones.

Follow the tracks of an old swamp raccoon and you will find that he has about three types of feeding on his mind—places which he will visit and inspect meticulously. First thought, once he is on the ground, is about those shallows and mudflats along the edge of the swamp. Here his nimble black fingers will probe all the likely places for frogs, freshwater mussels and crayfish. Each morsel of food is carefully washed before being eaten, except berries and other fruit. Even a frog which he has just snatched from a pond is carefully dunked before being eaten.

Trail sign of such raccoon activity is very apparent. You will see his tracks in the moist earth around ponds, flat distinctive prints, very much like tiny baby hands pressed into the mud. You will also see shells of mussels, clams and crayfish where he has shucked them out beside the pools.

The only way of hunting raccoon is with a pair of good coon hounds. These dogs must be smart, and they must love coon hunting as well as you do yourself in order to turn in a top performance. But the two in combination, good coon dogs and a smart old raccoon, will turn in an unbeatable night of hunting.

But just any dog will not do. There are certain distinctive traits which coon dogs must have. One is "bottom," as experienced raccoon hunters call it. "Bottom" is the measure of a coon dog's ability to take everything in the way of a complicated trail a smart, well seasoned raccoon lays down, and keep going hour after hour, finishing at the tree eager and full of fight.

There are two types of hounds for raccoon hunting. One, and perhaps the most important, is a slow methodical "strike" dog. This hound is used to pick up and work out the trail of none too fresh coon tracks, follow them until they are freshened up enough to put the quarry on the move. Once this happens, a good fast, open trailing hound is put down to crowd and force that raccoon to tree.

That strike is important. When you put down a strike dog, the act must be predicated on raccoon habit to be consistently successful. You must relate your hunt to available food and range and game habit. If there are cornfields with roasting ears reaching maturity, these are the places for your first cast. Put your strike dog down about ten o'clock in the evening, late enough so that the masked bandits raiding the corn fields have had time enough to work their way into this favored feeding range.

In such places you can cut your fast dog in almost at once, for the signs will be smoking fresh. Many raccoon hunters, in fact, will have just one reasonable fast dog with a keen nose, and will not use a strike dog at all, depending on their own ability to put down their dogs close to raccoon on the prowl. While this works reasonably well where the trail is hot, in the hunting of a wise old swamp coon, who moves much more at night, a slow methodical dog for the strike is almost a must.

Once a raccoon is jumped he has a bag full of tricks designed to fool even experienced hounds. Sometimes he will take to a river, swimming out in the current, as if to cross, then dropping downstream to come out on the same bank where he entered the water. At other times they will swim all the way across, touch the bank for a short distance to put down scent for the hounds, then return to the water. Not even the cleverest pack of hounds will tree all the raccoons they jump.

Even when a good fast pack of hounds forces one of those wise old swamp coons to take to a tree, he still has a few tricks he will use to confuse them. One, and the most misleading, is what experienced raccoon hunters call "tapping" a tree. A raccoon, pressed hard by hounds, will come up to a swamp oak, ash, or other tall growing tree and touch it, maybe run up the tree a short ways. Then he will come down, retrace his trail for several yards before taking to water. Sometimes, in retracing his trail, he will simply move back from the tree a hundred yards or so, then lay down a new trail toward more secure cover. By the time the hounds have unraveled his cross up trail, he is away with time to spare.

Truly great coon dogs know these characteristics of their quarry. Before a smart, experienced coon dog puts his stamp of approval on a treed coon by his mellow baying tree bark, he investigates thoroughly. It is amusing to watch him. He will carefully go over the base of the tree where a raccoon has touched it, his long nose aquiver with the pungency of fresh coon scent. Did this raccoon only "tap" the tree? Before giving his tree bark, a baying which is very distinct from his trailing voice, a smart experienced hound will circle the tree several yards out. He will take up his back trail and run it out for fifty yards or so, just to see that it is on the up and up.

If this methodical investigation tells him that no raccoon has left the tree, he makes endorsement of the fact with a long mellow tree bark.

Slower trailing hounds, coming up at this time, often make their own investigation before joining in with their treed bark.

But the pup out on his first few hunting trips, with plenty to learn about the quarry he is trailing, seldom has any thought of investigation. The smell of raccoon scent, the baying of other dogs is enough. If he has the makings of a future great raccoon dog in him, he is frantic about the tree, contributing more enthusiasm than judgment or ability to the hunt.

Eventually, those velvet soft ears will be scarred and torn from fighting raccoons. He will learn all the tricks of trailing and fighting from a master of the art—raccoon. Indeed, if one of those big swamp coons ever gets him in the water, you will be hard put to save him from being drowned, for a raccoon is the equal of any dog, regardless of experience, once battle is joined in the water.

Is there any special breed of hound who are superior coon dogs? The answer is a qualified no. I have yet to see a truly great raccoon hound which didn't have some Walker Fox Hound in his makeup. But by the same token I have seen excellent coon hounds with a bit of practically all other breeding in their makeup. Coon hounds, like razors, depend a lot more on the temper than on the brand. Like a great grouse dog, a great coon hound is usually the product of a great raccoon hunter.

Good raccoon hunters are perhaps the scarcest type of hunter found in game territory. You can find a hundred good hunters of other type game to one good raccoon hunter—a man who knows the habits of his quarry as well as he knows his own. Maybe it is the nocturnal habit of raccoons which accounts for this. But in large part it stems from the downright cleverness of the quarry itself.

What a teacher of woodcraft a raccoon is! Follow a couple of coon hounds trailing one of these masked bandits, jump him and tree him. The lesson in traveling, of keeping direction, is an education itself. Once you acquire the ability to roam the countryside at night, following coon hounds, the deer woods during daylight are comparatively easy.

One moment you are skirting a cornfield. The next moment you are away through the deep woods, so dark your light serves only to accent the gloom around you. But always, insistent and mellow, the baying of your hounds call you on. You will lose direction, the sense of time, but eventually you arrive at the tree where your quarry has taken refuge. Afterwards, with your hounds lying at your feet, panting from the trailing and final fight with the coon, you try to piece together the directions of your travel. Sometimes it will be an impossible task. But with experience you will begin to have a picture of your backtrail in reference to your present position. A compass will help in this, if you take occasional readings when you make drastic changes of course. Watch the skyline on ridges and hills outlined against the star studded night. In this way you learn the contours of your night country. But lost you will be occasionally—lost beyond any woods ability to set yourself straight before the coming of moonrise or morning. Go prepared for this.

Most of the essentials have been touched upon in Chapter 13, The Makings of a Small Game Hunter. A good light is always a requirement. The miner's carbide light, previously mentioned, is excellent for night walking, giving a bright flood lighting. In addition, you require a five cell flashlight to shine your game, once it is treed.

A rucksack with a lunch in it, a small handaxe, and a warm woolen jacket will put you on top of your hunt. It you have to spend a night in the woods you have the "makings" to do so.

I envy you on your first night afield after raccoons with some mellow voiced hounds setting the echoes ringing with their music and the frost jewels aglimmer on the stubble fields. It is a never to be forgotten experience.

Light side by side doubleguns are ideal for upland game. This is author's Richland Model 707, 20 ga., 28-inch barrels, very open improved cylinder right and very open modified left delivering 45 and 55 percent, respectively. Spreader loads open the patterns even more at 20 to 25-yard ranges where a lot of shots are offered.

CHAPTER 17

Hunting Ruffed Grouse

What is ruffed grouse cover? By that I mean ruffed grouse cover which produces more than an occasional bird—cover which has so many natural attractions that ruffed grouse naturally gravitate there. Something of the requirements were touched upon in Chapter 2, Basic Hunting. But that was merely relating these favored *game hot spots* for all hunting from cottontail, squirrel and ruffed grouse to deer. Here we are concerned with the requirements of ruffed grouse cover alone.

A successful ruffed grouse hunter must be able to pinpoint cover preferences within the over all favored sections. He must be able to recognize the happenstance of taking occasional birds outside these preferred spots for what it is, ruffed grouse actually outside their favored normal cover.

Breaking food requirements down into detail, here is what you come up with: wild grape; huckleberry; clover; tree buds; apples from abandoned apple orchards; wild fruit of opportunity, depending on the section; and abundance of worms and insects. You must consider these food requirements in relation to warmth, for the two are inseparable.

This warmth is found most constantly on the southern slopes, swales and valleys. Here the sun touches the cover constantly from early spring to late autumn. The wild harvest is always the heaviest here.

One section along a western river, where I fish steelhead during the summer, and hunt ruffed grouse in autumn, has wild grapes literally covering the maples and other trees, where the vines have reached up to the sun on these natural arbors. In late autumn, when the grapes are sun cured, ruffed grouse move in for the feasting. Other types of food which are abundant in this section, such as salmon berry seeds and salal berries, are but little used during the grape harvest.

When one eases along the banks of this beautiful river, which snakes its way through the coastal hills, the ruffed grouse concentrations are easily pin-pointed. It is not difficult to tell which section of river bank will afford shooting, and which section is scarcely worth hunting.

Where the river makes a turn, cutting off the southern exposure along a bank, the wild grape is less lush. It produces but little food, and that which it does produce is not the golden, dead-ripe grape like that of the side where the sun has had an opportunity to work its magic during a full growing season.

Just as my best shooting always occurred on those southern exposures of that winding river, it also occurs on the southern exposures of all hills in ruffed grouse territory, whether you are hunting in New England or on the West Coast.

Occasionally you will get a day's gunning which seemingly contradicts this. When you do, look for some reason why these birds have moved out of their favored cover. If you build a ruffed grouse finding philosophy on a few such instances, you are letting yourself in for a lot of fruitless tramping. The most deceptive occurrence is in finding ruffed grouse on low, cold damp ground, such as swamps.

Hunting such territory one day, I turned up an even half

dozen birds. The trees were dripping with the condensation of late autumn; the ground was cold and damp underfoot. Grouse cover? No. Those birds had been pushed out of their natural environment along the foothills by an army of hunters on opening day. The swampy section of their range was less hunted and they, like any other game, gravitated toward the security of this ill-favored section.

A good grouse woods is a mixed woods, with plenty of maples, beech, alder and such, but fairly well sprinkled with evergreens, too.

Evergreens are the shelter trees. Ruffed grouse use them for roosting, and for waiting out rough weather, except the severest storms. When a heavy blizzard occurs, ruffed grouse have the clever habit of flying directly into a snowdrift, sheltering snugly below the surface of the snow until the weather moderates.

But to get back to the texture of a ruffed grouse forest. Notice how, as the leaves fall along those south trending slopes, it becomes more open, letting in the late autumn sun? Notice, too, the dark leaf loam under the trees of a mixed forest? The hickory, hazel bushes, birch, beech, maple and alder produce a treasure of autumn leaves which is the delight of ruffed grouse and other leaf turning birds.

Al Lyman, hunter and philosopher, once remarked that you could tell good grouse territory by the feel of the soil. And that isn't as far down the ridge from the truth as it might first appear. When you add up the factors of good grouse cover: food and shelter, soil texture ties directly in with these two items.

Fallen leaves and the warmth of a south slope or swale combine to make a perfect environment for insects and worms which are a stable item of diet of ruffed grouse. Ever notice the leaf turning proclivities of birds in such places? Kick the leaves aside and you will see that the rick dark loam beneath carries a heavy complement of insect life. There is a seasonal cycle of activity here which not only makes such territory beautiful ruffed grouse habitat, but is also a wonderful environment for all wildlife.

Find any woods favored by other birds and you are touching upon potential ruffed grouse cover. Find any cover which doesn't carry its complement of other wildlife and you are hunting ruffed grouse in territory scarcely worth the effort.

Ruffed grouse is a creature of habit. When a hunter knows something of the reason behind his comings and goings, his hunting is much more interesting and productive. During the warm autumn days when the sun touches the south slopes with a mid-season warmth, he is very apt to be found dust bathing. Favored spots for this are old logging roads which have smoothed off the top soil leaving a spot of subsoil exposed to the sun. Such places are easily pin-pointed by the casual feathers found scattered about and the depressions in the dirt where ruffed grouse have lain.

These old roads are excellent places to hunt when working ruffed grouse cover. One such road which swings around a south facing hill near my cabin always produces a grouse or two when the autumn sun is shining. I often hunt along this road, without a dog, knowing just about the places which those ruffed grouse will use. Each season they will be found in these same places when conditions are right.

Habit also pin-points their roosting trees. One hemlock, within a half a mile of where this is written, shows the droppings of about three birds which use it constantly—even the same limbs are used for perching, as the droppings show. This roosting tree is one hundred yards down the slope from the top of a ridge. It is sheltered from the north winds here. In addition, its closely woven lattice of drooping limbs affords plenty of shelter in its own right by shedding water, sleet and snow.

It is no happenstance that those ruffed grouse use the south side of the tree for their roosting. They are interposing the bulk of that hemlock against the cold drag of air current which is always down slope during the night. See how it all adds up? From beginning to end the keys to the comings and goings of ruffed grouse are those primary ones of food, warmth and shelter.

Ruffed grouse, being lazy by nature, likes his home territory, too. He seldom roams much beyond the confines of his home thickets. Given plenty of foods, a few spots for dust bathing, proper shelter trees, and there is no incentive for him to abandon such cover. Once you find territory which has those requirements, cherish the knowledge and keep it secret, for you are sure of good ruffed grouse hunting in such cover, autumn after autumn.

There are two methods of hunting ruffed grouse—with a

Author's shotgun, an Over/Under 20 ga. Marlin, lower barrel straight cylinder, and upper barrel improved cylinder. This gun, handling size 7 shot in one ounce loadings, has excellent chokes for all short range upland shooting.

dog and without one. The latter method is more in keeping with stillhunting deer, though it does have a few twists individual to ruffed grouse hunting alone.

I love to hunt ruffed grouse without a dog—walking them up, as it is often called. Such hunting must be directly predicated on an intimate knowledge of grouse habit. You must know your game's reaction to your efforts to be at all successful.

Just recently I spent a full day stillhunting grouse in the cover where I normally prowl when looking for a big buck.

The similarity of such hunting is very apparent, though you may be armed with a shotgun for grouse or a rifle for deer.

This day it was cold and blustery, with the ruffed grouse holding close to the thickets. I eased along convenient deer trails, watching the cover ahead for some movement of my quarry, listening for the small talk which ruffed grouse usually make before flushing. Once I touched off a big five point buck in a clump of laurel. Again, it was a doe I jumped instead of grouse. Eventually, after an hour of careful hunting, I touched cover which held ruffed grouse.

First ruffed grouse I flushed spiraled out of the alders without giving me a chance for a shot. I marked the direction it took when it leveld off, confident that I could again walk it up within shotgun range.

It is characteristic of ruffed grouse to continue on in the direction they flush without any great amount of deviation. Once you put one up, it is very apt to be found in the cover some hundred yards or so in the general direction it was taking when you first marked it. This one angled along the ridge, keeping just enough below the top to stay within the sheltering belt of those southern slopes and away from the bite of the bitter north wind.

I worked down-slope a bit in order to be slightly below my game when I flushed it. I eased through a thimbleberry thicket, pausing frequently to watch the cover ahead. I walked up two more ruffed grouse, getting one as it crossed a small opening in the alders, missing the other on a quartering shot which appeared deceptively easy. Afterwards, I flushed a lone ruffed grouse in the cover where my first bird disappeared, and took it with a snapshot on a straightaway try.

I like to hear ruffed grouse talk, the nervous chatter they make before flushing, but quite often in hunting them by walking, the first intimation you have of their presence is the heart stopping thunder of wings as they explode out of the autumn leaves which blend so beautifully with their own rich coloring.

Working ruffed grouse with a dog has an attraction for upland gunners seldom found in any other type of shotgunning. Even quail are unable to hold hunters like ruffed grouse. One such hunter once told me, "Gimme a week in ruffed grouse cover with a good Irish Setter, and I can get by the rest of the year."

An Irish Setter and ruffed grouse *are* unbeatable, it seems to me. Many experienced gunners say that there is no other ruffed grouse dog quite like an Irish Setter. In fact those truly great ruffed grouse dogs I have known have all been Irishers. Yet when I say that, I must make room for a Springer Spaniel with which I hunted everything from duck to ruffed grouse. Bob was that kind of dog. He had the knack of anticipating your own hunting strategy, as well as just about knowing what your game would do.

It seemed to me he patterned his hunting according to the game reaction to the weather. On those cold, clear days, when the cover was noisy, the grouse flushing wild, he hunted carefully, slowly, touching the cover with a delicacy which put the birds up within range. On those blustery days, when they held close to the thickets, he ranged faster, crashed the thickets to send them thundering out to your gun.

Characteristics of this nature in a hunting dog are not exactly brought about by training. They are more the results of letting a good intelligent dog develop his own natural peculiarities of hunting—within reason. Training which fosters such characteristics has as its basis a very close relationship between the hunter and his dog. When your dog shows by this action that he has the mark of a truly great ruffed grouse dog, encourage it by praise for his good work afield.

Many grouse hunters swear by a good pointer as being the ultimate in ruffed grouse dogs. And such dogs are beautiful to see, working the cover with a very light touch, when properly trained to this king of all game birds.

Again, it simmers down to the individual dog. My first choice is a setter. But thousands of hunters would disagree with me. In fact the trend is toward pointers. Probably more pointers are used on ruffed grouse now than any other breed of dog.

Any breed, however, can be trained to hunt ruffed grouse —if the dog has it in him, and this is complemented by careful, understanding and training. As he progresses, he will learn to love ruffed grouse hunting above all else. He will develop peculiarities of hunting, which, as I have said, must be fostered.

It might be said, and I believe truthfully, that ruffed grouse also develop certain peculiarities in hunters. You either love ruffed grouse or you are not a ruffed grouse hunter.

CHAPTER 18

Squirrel Hunting

Early American backwoodsmen took squirrel with their long barreled flint-lock rifles by aiming at the bark of the tree directly beneath a squirrel's head, the concussion of the ball killing their quarry without leaving a mark. They brought an uncanny ability to the simple task of shooting a mess of squirrels. But this shooting skill alone wasn't the greater part of their hunting ability. The knack of reading sign and clever still-hunting, made an even greater contribution to their squirrel hunting.

Sure, game was much more plentiful in those days. One could find plenty of squirrel in any hardwood forest. But it was hunting ability which put them within the short ranges necessary for such shooting. It was woodcraft which gave them shots at completely stationary targets.

Squirrel hunting is predicated on several factors which a hunter must meet satisfactorily to be successful. Foremost is the matter of suitable habitat. There is never a uniform population of squirrel or other game in a forest. Some sections will be totally barren of wildlife, from the smallest leaf turning birds, ruffed grouse and rabbit, to deer and elk. What constitutes good grouse cover is also good squirrel hunting territory.

Take, for example, the question of food. Call the roll of suitable nut and fruit producing trees and vines and you come up with a mixed forest—chestnut, walnut, oak, elderberry, huckleberry and wild grape. Sounds like beautiful ruffed grouse territory, doesn't it? Also sounds like a nice place to finagle a big buck later in the autumn—and it is. Such trees attract a complement of squirrel and other game.

My squirrel hunting is done mostly in oak groves, and my principal quarry is gray squirrel. Occasionally I spend a day hunting pine or red squirrel. But regardless of specie, and there are over thirty-five on the North American continent, the problem of food, shelter and desirable range are essentially the same.

First bit of evidence of squirrel a woodsman usually finds are "cuttings"—shell of acorns, and nuts where fox squirrel or a gray have shucked out the sweet meated nut and left the refuge around the base of a tree where they have worked. In western forests, red squirrel frequently give evidence of their presence by leaving pine and fir cone shuckings. Such sign is obvious, easily seen by the most inexperienced hunter, but it is the simple beginning of successful squirrel hunting. It is the start of the hunt.

The task of approaching likely squirrel territory, however, and making sure by the evidence left that it is worth hunting, is comparable to the ability of finding and evaluating suitable deer cover.

There are also several parallels in the hunting. When still-hunting squirrel you must be able to pin-point their activities by relating them to the time of day you are hunting. Like deer, the greatest activity of squirrels occurs in the fore part of the day. During midday they are less active, though there is always some movement, nut cutting and such.

The most rewarding thing a squirrel hunter can do is to move into active territory, sit down where he can have two or three nut trees under observation, then wait it out. In this you have many of the elements of trail watching for deer. You must bring the same concentration to the task. You must remain perfectly quiet for an hour—better make it a half day. Study the normal activities of squirrel, their quarreling and their nut gathering. At the end of the period you will have a very good concept of not only squirrel activity, but forest activity in general. Forests are noisy places, bustling with activities, if you but wait patiently where you may watch and listen.

Movement, especially the unstudied movements and sounds of an inexperienced hunter, cancel out woodland activity. An inexperienced woodsman progresses through the cover convinced that it is deserted. But if he could see and hear the activity before his own noisy cross country hiking cancels it out, or if he could see and hear this activity after his passage, he would be much more circumspect in his comings and goings.

Is there any one type of movement which is less alarming to game than average hunter sound and movement? I believe there is. In fact I believe that the entire concept of stalking must be predicated on movement and sound which is not alarming to game.

If every squirrel within hearing took to a den tree at the snap of a twig, if ruffed grouse flushed wildly for the same reason and deer crashed away at the first sound of a soft-footed hunter on a game trail, then little if any game would be taken by stillhunting.

No game, from the largest to the smallest are frightened by familiar movements or sound. They are alerted, surely. They take precautions, too. But they wait it out for more confirming evidence before committing themselves to action.

What movement and sound is most familiar to squirrels and other small game? Most obvious sound, other than their own, is that of larger game. During the early morning hours when squirrels, grouse and other small game are actively feeding, big game is also on the move. A hunter easing through a woodland at this time, taking it quietly, moving slowly, very closely duplicates the action and sounds of big game. He will get in much closer on squirrels or grouse before the game be-

comes alarmed. It is at such times that he will get his best opportunities for shooting.

This as a hunting concept is so radical it must be tested by
the average hunter before he believes it possible. But it has
worked with any number of experienced hunters. Predators,
such as fox, coyote and bobcat know this peculiarity of the
game they stalk. Their hunting is done at the time of greatest
game activity, not only because they have more opportunities
at this time, but also because movement and noise are the
least noticed at this time.

They capitalize on this sure knowledge by confining their
hunting mostly to those early morning and late afternoon
hours when game is on the move. Sure, bobcat occasionally
take roosting grouse at night. Other predators are also on the
prowl at this time, but their usual quarry are nocturnal, and
such hunting also comes at the peak of night activity.

Hunting squirrels with a dog is a very common method of
taking the bushy-tails. In such hunting, the mixed breed of
dog, the small mutt comes into its own. Ten chances to one
that the neighborhood mongrel has the makings of a good
squirrel dog.

What is a good squirrel dog? What is he expected to do,
tree squirrels and track them on the ground? All this and
something else—an intangible above the requirements usually
associated with game-running dogs. Again, this is something
which the individual mutt is very apt to develop on his own.

I once had a small dog, Pete of undetermined ancestry,
though he had indications of fox terrier and Boston bull in his
makeup. Pete was a beautiful working squirrel dog. No one
trained him, but he had the habit of following me afield when
I hunted gray squirrels. When I found good squirrel territory
and sat down, Pete would also sit down beside me, one ear
cocked, quietly listening and watching. And it was he who
usually spotted a squirrel. There would come a gentle tapping
of his tail on the leaves. I would turn to see where he was
looking, and usually I spotted our quarry. After the shot he
would walk over and retrieve our game, then return to his
watching. In ten minutes or a half hour the squirrels would
resume their feeding. Then that gentle rapping of Pete's tail
would begin again, and there would be another gray. He was
unfailing in his watching. And he never made a mistake. A
squirrel ever so high in a ridge oak was easily pin-pointed by

Pete, even though all he had to go by was some movement of the branches or leaves against the wind. Sometimes I questioned his judgment, but if I watched and waited long enough, a squirrel would materialize in the oak he was watching.

Squirrel watching wasn't Pete's only hunting ability. When I tried walking them up during the acorn harvest, a time when the most squirrels are found on the ground, he would gently nudge through the underbrush. His careful, slow working of the cover always took those squirrels by surprise. They would scamper up a tree to the first limb, then pause to scold and curse Pete. But not a word would they get out of him in reply. Pete waited, unmoving, until I made the shot. If it was a miss he showed his disappointment by leaving the tree; if I made a hit, he would bring my squirrel to me.

Squirrel dogs should range close and slow. And if you find one which is not a loud tree barker, cherish him above all things. For there is nothing which will cancel out woodland activity like a loud-mouthed squirrel dog.

The silent tree dog will become lost from you occasionally, and you must hunt him up. But that is much better than having him advertise his presence at the tree by loud continued barking.

There is one characteristic of squirrel when hunted with dogs that is sometimes confusing. That is the habit of slipping around the tree, away from the side on which the dog is watching. This is especially evident when you are hunting with a noisy dog. I think it is also very much more apt to occur when you are using a dog of large size. Smaller dogs, such as Pete, seem to arouse more resentment than caution in squirrels. Sometimes this characteristic occurs when you are stillhunting.

Such a game of hide and seek can be exasperating, especially when the squirrel moves just enough to keep out of sight when you circle the tree. My hunting friend Elzie Randolph, who learned his squirrel hunting in the river bottom lands of Oklahoma, had a very neat rick to frustrate those smart fox squirrels which were his usual quarry in that section. To bring a squirrel around to his side of the tree, he would wait for a few minutes. Then, about the time his squirrel began to wonder what had become of him, he would toss a stick around to the other side of the tree. Immediately there would be a scurrying in top of the tree, and his quarry would appear, sure that he was putting the tree between him and the hunter beneath.

Such tricks pay off in squirrel hunting. There are other payoffs all along the line. I doubt if there is a better way of becoming familiar with woods, and all woods hunting. That is why I believe that no one is a finished big game hunter who hasn't served an apprenticeship hunting squirrels.

CHAPTER 19

Woodchuck Hunting

Here is game of the open pastures. Here is game that can live under a farmer's barn, raid his garden season after season and live high, despite the best efforts of the landowner to lay him by the heels. Woodchuck hunting is all things to all outdoorsmen. It has many of the elements of long range big game shooting, such as mule deer and elk in the more open western mountains. At times the ranges at which he is taken are more in keeping with the whitetail deer ranges of eastern and northern hunting.

You can hunt him with a .22 rimfire, taking out in stalking what your rifle lacks in killing power and flat trajectory. You can utilize a long range sniping outfit costing around $500 and the woodchuck will match its accuracy and range in every particular.

Once, when I was living in the mountains of western Washington, I spent the spare time at two summers hunting woodchuck with handguns. Mind you, these were the famed rockchucks, the ideal target of long range riflemen. We stalked them among the rocks near timberline, the hunting being pleasant breaks in our fishing excursions to those high Alpine lakes.

"Whistlers," we called them. But by any name, they were woodchuck—always willing and able to play the game according to the rules you yourself made. Hunt them with handguns, .22 rifles or long range sniping rifles, they always turn in a good performance.

Just recently a chuck hunter from Colorado told me that

unless you could take them consistently at two and three hundred yards, your bag would be mighty slim in the Rockies where he hunted. A steelhead angler from the Middle West, fishing the same riffle on the Rogue River in southwestern Oregon, said, "Shucks, I hunt whistle pigs back home with a shotgun along the edge of my hay fields." His eyes lit up with the memory. "Sporting targets they are, too."

What type of game is this which occupies such a wide variety of habitat, and is hunted in so many different ways? If he exemplifies the type of shooting associated with long range big game hunting, how is it people knock him rolling with a shotgun or handgun?

The hunting to which he is subjected is part of the answer. The type of territory in which he is found is also a consideration. A New England woodchuck, which has had his wits sharpened by constant sniping through several seasons, is a very skeptical creature. He is not the woodchuck of Midwestern hayfields that allows himself to be taken with a shotgun. Dumb woodchuck just do not grow up in New England meadows. Somebody picks them off before their distrust of movement way out there at one and two hundred yards has solidified into a permanent livable philosophy.

Let's take a look at such a wise, suspicious woodchuck, grown fat on the clover of his hillside home grounds. First thing you notice is his chunkiness. Lift one and you will be surprised at his weight. Here is a nice sized target. You wonder how it is possible to miss him at reasonable ranges.

His color is grizzly-brown, though a jet black chuck is not too uncommon. Generally, however, his coat is that grizzly-brown which blends in well with just about any background from young spring clover to the copper tarnish of August stubble fields.

His dens and burrows are easily located by sight, and, it must be added, by their odors as well. He prefers well drained ground for his diggings, and once this is found, he usually digs a very intricate burrow with two or more entrances. Here, during the cold winter months, "the hunger time" as the Indians call it, he will snooze away the cold stormy days, snug in his burrow, living off that fat which has accumulated on his ample frame during spring and summer.

At one time woodchuck were considered more a forest animal in the eastern part of his range. He fed on the tender bark and roots of various kinds. But now he finds it much more to the point living close to cultivated fields where he can do his raiding without too much effort.

Best shooting time is late evening and early morning when he is more apt to be caught actively foraging well away from his den.

During early spring, when he first emerges from hibernation, he is a trifle less cautious than he will be later, affording a bit more short range snapshooting.

Is off-hand snapshooting a hard field position for you to master? If so, do as I know one woodchuck hunter near Klamath Falls Oregon does; he hunts rockchuck with his deer rifle, taking no shots except from an off-hand position. He also had trouble with his off-hand position while big game hunting. He was missing too many of those big, old, gray-faced muley bucks in the Gearhart Mountains, so he turned to off-season woodchuck shooting with this specific problem in mind.

How well he solved it was exemplified one day in late autumn when I met him on a deer hunting trip. I stood beside him that day when another hunter spooked a mule deer buck out of a jackpine thicket. It came crashing out on a dead run, getting into the clear with about four jumps before this hunter sent it end over end with a neck shot. Range? Seventy-five yards. But don't let that short distance detract from the accuracy of the shot, or the downright shooting skill required to make it.

Later, around my campfire that night we talked of hunting. Not deer, but woodchuck hunting. This hunter said that he fired five hundred handloads at rockchuck each summer, at ranges from fifty to two hundred yards. He averaged around one hundred fifty chucks each season. On the lava beds where he picked them off, it was either a clean killing hit or miss, because a touch was sufficient to blow them up with his 270 Winchester, using 100 grain bullets.

While all this shooting was done off-hand, a day's hunt gave him just about every type shot in the book, from running to standing. It reminded me very much of the type shooting Art Richardson and I obtained while hunting ground squirrel. (Chapter 1, Plinking With A Purpose).

Off-hand field shooting comprises at least ninety percent of all deer and elk shooting. And this hunter spent his off-season shooting time polishing his technique for the type of shot he would normally get when hunting mule deer in the Gearharts.

He would ease along through the lava buttes, watching for rockchuck sunning themselves on the ledges, or feeding on the sparse grass and browse. Of course there were elements of mule deer hunting in this other than that all important off-hand shooting. Both place a premium on quiet going. The type of shot he got was directly tied in with his ability as a still-hunter and stalker. Whether those rockchuck would be scurrying for their dens in the rimrocks, or waiting out the shot depended on how he hunted, the skill he brought to the stalking.

Woodchuck hunting is not alone an excellent place to develop off-hand shooting skills. Most woodchuck shooting has a lot in common with long range big game shooting. Taking woodchuck during the latter part of summer, when they have had their wits sharpened by constant gunning for several months, is definitely not a short range affair. It is tied in directly with open range, big game hunting. Here is no underslung target to be taken off-hand at fifty to a hundred yards.

Heavily hunted woodchuck (and ground squirrel) will spook at unbelievable distances. Shooting them is a superb test of marksmanship. You must be able to dope wind; you must be able to read and know the effect of mirage shimmer-

Rangematic Mark V rangefinder—useful in both small and big game hunting. It contains a 6 x 18 scope which can be removed for separate use, spotting game, sporting events, etc.

ing between you and your intended target. Above all, your sight picture and range picture must be on the button for a clean kill (Chapter 3, Sight Picture Is Not Enough).

All this adds up to long range elk shooting, mountain hunting and mule deer hunting in the breaks and rimrocks of western mountains. No one is prepared for long range big game hunting unless he has spent several summer sessions, either with woodchuck or its West Coast understudy, ground squirrel. Such shooting rounds out your ability as a big game shot.

Woodchuck is a wonderful game animal in his own right, but a rifleman gets more pleasure out of his woodchuck hunting when he is shaping up his hunting skills toward the ultimate end of going big game hunting.

CHAPTER 20

Going Deer Hunting?

Deer is the most prevalent big game in the United States. Its range is extensive, and for every type of deer hunting, from long range mule deer shooting, to the hunting of eastern whitetail deer in heavy cover, it has its counterpart in small game hunting of some type. It is the logical outgrowth of those days spent afield after rabbit, squirrel and grouse. There comes a time when the small game hunter naturally turns to big game. It is the testing ground of all the woodcraft he has learned and his ability with a rifle.

Let's take an excursion into typical deer cover, such as is found in a great deal of the west, north and eastern deer forests. These are not strange woods to a small game hunter. Fact is, it is very typical of squirrel, snowshoe rabbit and grouse cover. Perhaps while hunting small game you have come to a depression under a hemlock where a large animal has bedded. As you probably know, this was a deer. Look at it closely. Not much to read from this actual impression in the autumn leaves, is there? Perhaps you had better take another look. After all, when you found evidence of squirrel cuttings under the oaks, you developed your hunt from *that* small beginning, didn't you?

Remember how it was—just a few acorn cuttings on a moss-grown log. You eased along the ridge, farther into the grove. Then you saw your first game, a beautiful gray squirrel near the top of a wide spreading oak. The rest was easy. You finished the day with four squirrel—and you developed your entire hunt because you read signs correctly.

This deer bed, sheltered from the rain and snow, has a lot to tell a deer hunter, too. First question a hunter wants to know is how fresh is this sign, for it may be the beginning of a successful deer hunt, just as those acorn cuttings were the beginning of a successful day of squirrel hunting.

See where the leaves are scuffed up, how the brown soil shows beneath, as though it has been freshly turned? Notice how the forest litter is pressed flat directly in the bed, and hasn't sprung up again? Place your hand in the depression. Feel the warmth? When you angled up across the draw below, this deer probably left its bed. Before that he had heard you, traced your progress by the noise you made. But he was uncertain about the necessity of leaving his bed until you crossed the draw and turned up-slope.

You had him fooled up to that point. Your progress was that of unalarmed game—slow movement, a pause to scan the cover, slow movement again. The sound which he heard was that of a cautious deer moving in the cover. But when you crossed the draw below him, a thermal winddrift, moving uphill at this time of day, brought hunter scent to his keen inquisitive nose. He slipped out and left his bed for you to ponder.

A trained woodsman, reading the evidence would know a lot about the deer that made it. He would relate it to *available feeding areas* in the neighborhood. He would scout the cover for evidence of game movement in and out of this security-cover where he found the bed. By the time he was through his investigation, he would know where his game was feeding, on what type food it was presently feeding, as well as how many other deer were with this one which made the bed under the hemlock.

Deer are secretive. They will spend time raiding farm gardens, grain fields and clover meadows, slipping in and out of their hideaways without betraying their presence to the irate farmer. Here in the dust of a farm lane will be seen the blunt toed tracks of a big deer, probably a buck. Here also will be found the smaller, slender tracks of lesser deer.

Maybe, some early morning or late evening they will be seen slipping along toward their feeding grounds. But in the more open feeding ranges of settled farm communities, they tend to become nocturnal. They quit feeding before good shooting light in the mornings. They only come out to feed in late evening after good shooting light is past. Once they have fed to repletion, during the night their day-bedding will be found in some secretive place where they can keep a collective eye and nose on their security.

So tracks and beddings are the average hunter's introduction to deer, especially eastern whitetail and West Coast blacktail deer. Tracks at first glance seem to be made without rhyme or reason; beds seem to be placed without consideration of feeding and security cover, but once deer habits are more thoroughly understood, both tracks and beddings make sense. Like small game hunting, the basic premise of deer hunting is simply this: *nothing is done without purpose*. Even the most casual track of a deer has some over-all significance that ties in directly with your big game hunt.

When you walk through a woods looking for sign of game, what is it that first attracts your attention? It is *cover which has been disturbed* in some manner—ferns turned back to expose the undersides, branches which have been touched and have dropped their burdens of snow, bright red underbark of cedar, mountain willow, alder, showing deer "rubbings" or bushes hooked and broken by pugnacious bucks in autumn.

See what excellent training you had while small game hunting? There sign reading was just as essential as it is now when you are hunting deer. Deer sign is more obvious than that of squirrel, rabbit or ruffed grouse, but it is basically the same—cover which has been disturbed in some respect.

How fresh is the sign? Again, you apply the yardstick of small game sign-reading. Fresh ruffed grouse sign such as the leaf turning and scratching, age at the same rate as deer tracks. In each case, dark fresh earth is exposed, and this is subjected to the same amount of weathering. Sun turns it grey. Rain beats it down, forming a surface crust which is quite apparent to even the most inexperienced hunter. Snowfall easily pin-points sign by erasing older evidence, leaving the cover like a clean slate for identification of the new sign.

There are three methods of hunting deer: trail watching, driving and still-hunting, though these three types of hunting are actually divisions of still-hunting.

Take a look at the first two methods in connection with your squirrel hunting. They tie in directly with the most successful techniques which you used on those bushy-tails. Fact is, there is no better place to learn the fine art of deer trail watching than waiting out the many squirrel hunting situations with which you are confronted in typical squirrel woods. It teaches you the importance of patience, of taking it easy. It shows you how often any hunting situation is improved by just waiting quietly for the hunt to develop.

Trail watching for deer is done on runways, natural passes, and escape routes through which game normally move when flushed from security-cover, or in going from one section of cover to another. When an army of hunters are on the prowl, they keep the game moving. Hunters who are most successful are those who have made a careful study of the section in which they plan to hunt, and have selected watching spots where they can intercept game jumped by other hunters.

That would seem like an almost impossible task if it wasn't for the habit of deer using about the same trails and woodland passes in their comings and goings. This phase of big game hunting is very extensively treated in my book *The Art of Successful Deer Hunting.* Here it is touched upon only to show the relationship between this type of hunting and some phases of small game hunting.

In stillhunting deer, the problem of moving through heavy cover is essentially that encountered when stillhunting cottontail rabbit, snowshoe rabbit or squirrel. There is no distinct technique which is good, basically, for hunting rabbit and not good for other game.

Even at the expense of reiteration, the basic consideration in all cases is slow, careful movement. It is movement of a type which game find familiar, both from the standpoint of sound and rate of progress through the cover.

You, as an experienced squirrel hunter, know these things and practice them instinctively. (Chapter 19, Squirrel Hunting). Stillhunting techniques, such as this, have further application in driving game, such as deer. When you are on a deer stand you are a stillhunter; you are a stillhunter when you trail watch for game.

This important attribute of all hunting is intangibly grounded in proper hunter attitude—carefulness and acute knowledge of game reaction to hunting.

You cannot move around a stand, making loud noises, coughing, stamping to restore circulation, and expect game to be moved across your gunning position. You must wait as inconspicuously as if you were watching for gray squirrel. You must be alert for the snap of a twig, the switch of grey and soft bodies pressed against the cover, for this will probably be your first intimation of the deer's approach. Of course you are not going to train your rifle on this sound or movement, for that is criminally stupid, but it will warn you to be ready when fair game breaks into an opening.

I actually have known inexperienced hunters who let deer cross stands on which they were posted without seeing them! They hadn't realized the importance of studying the stand, in selecting a spot from which to watch. They had left "blind spots" in their stands places which they couldn't cover. Later, when drivers pushed a big buck across, the deer took the most logical direction, threading its way up a small draw in

In the woods stillhunting—soft-finish clothing will not make noise spooking game and all items carried, including those in rucksack, see service often enough to be classified as indispensable.

one case, which afforded concealment, past the unsuspecting stander, and into the security-cover beyond the stand. It was all there in the snow, plain sign reading, even the spot where the big deer, unquestionably a buck, paused to look back in the direction of the posted hunter.

A small game hunter who has studied the best possible

crossing to post when running either snowshoe or cottontail rabbit with hounds, has had this problem emphasized time after time. I am betting *he* wouldn't have taken up his position on that deer stand quite so casually. He would have known the importance of studying it in reference to his expected shooting.

If deer stands, like rabbit stands, are selected properly, the natural exit areas posted between the territory you plan to drive and the next security-cover, you will have little trouble moving them across your posting. Posting wrong, or driving wrong, only make for disappointment. Just remember, you cannot drive them out into inhospitable openings just because such places afford good shooting. There must be some attraction beyond the stand toward which they would logically move when put out.

Deer shooting in heavy cover, snapshooting as it is called, is perhaps the most difficult field shooting to learn, and at the same time, once this shooting is mastered, it is the most productive. It is difficult for the beginning deer hunter because the type of shooting is completely foreign to anything he has done in the past—unless he is an avid small game hunter. Then it is easy. Snapshooting of deer is essentially no different than snapshooting a cottontail smoking across an opening between bits of cover. And that goes whether you are using a shotgun or rifle.

You have the same problem of a moving target. You have the same element of limited time in which to get off the shot. These two factors tend to do one of two things to a hunter. They either cause him to develop a fast rhythmical manner of mounting his rifle and getting off his shot, or they totally confuse him, reduce his shooting technique to a "yank and chance it" manner of shooting which is both inaccurate and comparatively slow.

Small game shooting techniques, which have been emphasized throughout this book, are tops for deer shooting. Actual snapshooting techniques as applied to deer shooting are quite thoroughly discussed in my book, *The Art of Successful Deer Hunting.* It is sufficient here to point out the similarity of such shooting.

A small game hunter brings all this experience, plus a keen woodcraft, to the golden hours he will spend deer hunting. Never mind if you have never taken a buck, you already know more about the actual hunting of deer than many hunters who have made two or three kills. What is more, when you do down your buck, the event will be based on hunting know-how, not luck. It is the logical outgrowth of those many times you were out after cottontail, woodchuck, ground squirrels, snowshoe rabbits, grouse or raccoon.

Not every deer hunter is lucky enough to bag a deer with a rack like this! To improve the odds, stay in practice during the off-seasons with a .22 counterpart to your deer rifle.